THE ORIGIN OF THE KINGDONS

THE ORIGIN OF THE KINGDONS

R. D. Kingdon

BROWN DOG BOOKS

Published under licence by Brown Dog Books and
The Self-Publishing Partnership, 7 Green Park Station, Bath BA1 1JB

www.selfpublishingpartnership.co.uk

978-1-78545-162-1

Cover design by Kevin Rylands
Internal design by Andrew Easton

Printed and bound by CPI Group (UK) Ltd, Croydon CR0 4YY

For DNK and ADNK

Foreword

In this essay I describe the origin of the Kingdons: who they were, where they came from, what they did, why they did it, and how they relate to their present-day namesakes. My double use of the definite article is deliberate: what I describe is, indeed, *the* origin (singular) of *the* Kingdons (also singular, taken as a family group). This unequivocal statement makes an implicit claim to truth which, if it is to be believed, must be substantiated 'beyond reasonable doubt' from records that are known to be reliable. It also presumes a number of caveats that restrict its scope. These supporting arguments and delimiting constraints will be discussed later; but first I will set out the key facts and events that constitute what is known of the early history of the Kingdons. It's quite a story.

Narrative

The family name now spelt K-i-n-g-d-o-n was first adopted in the thirteenth century by the inhabitants of a farm now known as Kendon, which is on the east side of Dartmoor in Devon.[1] The name of the farm is derived from the Old English words for 'king' and 'hill'; and indeed the farm is located on the side of a hill that is surmounted by a natural jumble of rocks known as King Tor, and a Bronze Age burial cairn known as King's Barrow.[2] The earliest verified instance of this usage is in the record of a plea at the Devon eyre of 1244 by Walter de Kyngdon and Orresia his wife.[3] They were the very first 'of Kyngdon', for the simple reason that Orresia had been given this homestead by her father as part of her marriage portion.[4] In medieval times a gift of real estate to a daughter was quite unprecedented, and in this case it was not allowed to pass without an equally unusual challenge in the courts of law. The controversy was exacerbated by the fact that Kendon had been part of an estate of land held by the same Anglo-Saxon family since before the Norman Conquest; and so it would have remained if not for the fact that Orresia's brother had been outlawed for murder.

1 See map, Figure 1. Also note that, for the purpose of this narrative, I have maintained a single spelling for each person or place, notwithstanding the wide variation in the historical record and in common use. By spelling the generic family name 'Kingdon' I am following the convention established by [Kingdon Family] p.1.

2 See cover photographs.

3 See scan, Figure 2.

4 [Devon Eyre 1238] p.97 n.595. In the interests of readability I have tried to avoid cluttering this narrative with a surfeit of references, particularly in support of the more general observations. Nevertheless there are many specific points that have been gleaned from unique and little-known records, such as this reference to Orresia's marriage portion, and for each of these I have given the source.

For the full story, it is necessary to go back to the earliest known record of the landholding of which Kendon had been a part, which appears in the Domesday Book of 1086.

Following the Norman Conquest in 1066, England was occupied by a military regime that exercised close control through a rigorous implementation of the feudal system. For the first time, no estate of land was owned outright save by the king, who owned everything. That is, every landholder became a tenant answerable to an overlord. For the vast majority of the 'English' – the Anglo-Saxons whose ancestors themselves had forcefully occupied the land some six centuries before – the Norman Conquest meant that they owed homage and dues to a foreigner whose only qualification was that he happened to be on the winning side. Orresia's ancestor was not like the vast majority of the English, however. As recorded in the Domesday Book, Ælfric of Shapley and Skerraton was one of just fourteen English thanes of the king who held lands in Devon both before and after the Conquest.[5] To be a 'thane of the king' meant that a landholder owed homage and dues directly to the king: a degree of access and proximity that must have been seen as a privilege of considerable distinction. As for the payment of dues, in the case of Ælfric and his descendants this mainly comprised the service of contributing two or three arrows whenever the king came to hunt on Dartmoor, which doesn't seem at all onerous. In all other respects the family could continue as before, generation after generation, just as long as they obeyed the law, and as long as each successive patriarch fathered a legitimate male heir. Such royal magnanimity perhaps explains the Kingdon family motto, *Regis donum gratum bonum*, expressing gratitude for the king's good gift.[6]

I have noted that Orresia's ancestor Ælfric was 'of Shapley and Skerraton'. Shapley is an old name for a region of North Bovey parish that includes the adjacent farmsteads of Kendon and South Hookner, both of which were held by Ælfric; it is not to be confused with Shapley in the nearby parish of Chagford. Skerraton is a farm in Dean Prior parish, a dozen miles south of Kendon; it is not to be confused with Scorriton in the nearby parish of West Buckfastleigh. Did Ælfric hold any other lands

---

5 This and subsequent Domesday Book statistics have been derived from [Domesday] in conjunction with [Domesday Devon Notes] n.52.

6 [Kingdon Family] p.131; [Kingdon Family Second Look] p.77.

TRE?[7] We may never know the answer to this question, because of the dearth of reliable records, and because in this case even the Domesday Book adds nothing but muddle and confusion by failing to differentiate between the many Englishmen named Ælfric. The Domesday survey identifies 272 distinct estates of land that were held by Ælfric TRE, thirty-three of them (including Shapley and Skerraton) in Devon alone.[8] In the absence of further evidence it is impossible to know whether Orresia's ancestor Ælfric held any of these estates in addition to Shapley and Skerraton. All we can say is that the Ælfric who held Shapley and Skerraton TRE also held Shapley and Skerraton at the time of the Domesday survey, that is, roughly twenty years later. Incidentally, from the 272 distinct estates of land that were held by Ælfric TRE, just six of them (including Shapley and Skerraton) were held as tenant-in-chief by the same person after the Conquest: a stark illustration of the catastrophic dispossession suffered by the English, and of the rarity of the privilege enjoyed by Ælfric of Shapley and Skerraton.

Between Ælfric of Shapley and Skerraton in 1086 and his descendant Orresia in 1244 there is a gap of 158 years, that is, five or six intermediate generations. Of these intermediaries only one can be identified with any certainty: Orresia's father, David of Shapley and Skerraton. However, the fact that David's dual landholding was identical to Ælfric's is a strong indication that he was a direct descendant. Moreover, a contemporary record in the Devon Book of Fees states that David held his lands 'by the service of finding 2 arrows whenever our lord the King comes to hunt in the forest of Dertemore and his ancestors since the Conquest held upon these terms.'[9] So perhaps this is sufficient to establish the lineage.

In an attempt to identify an earlier David, who had witnessed a twelfth-century charter granting lands to Buckfast Abbey, Dom Adam Hamilton conjectures that he was 'probably the royal huntsman, whose descendants held land not far from Buckfast, by the service of providing the king with arrows when he went to hunt on Dartmoor, name and office

7 The Domesday Book acronym TRE stands for *Tempore Regis Eduardi*, that is, in the time of King Edward the Confessor, just before the Conquest.
8 This statistic is for landholders identified simply as 'Ælfric', that is, it excludes the holdings of Ælfric Blaec, Ælfric Kemp, Ælfric Mouse, Ælfric Small, and so on.
9 [Devon Book of Fees] p.423 n.1371.

being seemingly hereditary'.[10] This is not as far-fetched as it sounds. Firstly, in medieval England the name 'David' was quite unusual, being neither Anglo-Saxon nor Norman but from the Bible. Maybe Ælfric felt that his successors should evince complete neutrality, and that the Biblical David was an appropriate model, as he had been the king's armour-bearer, skilled with the slingshot, and adept at dodging arrows.[11] Secondly, David being such an unusual name, there couldn't have been many of them in the vicinity of Buckfast Abbey in the twelfth century; at least, not so many as to induce the earlier David to qualify his name with his location or profession. So perhaps Hamilton is on to something. And he may not be far from the mark when he identifies the hereditary office of 'royal huntsman', for Ælfric was unique amongst the king's English thanes in holding land on Dartmoor. His closest rival was Aldred brother of Odo, who held land in Manaton; but Aldred had another title, 'the forester', which presumably excluded him for being the 'royal huntsman' as well. On the other hand, for many years prior to disafforestation in 1204 the whole of Devon was under forest law, so having expert local knowledge of Dartmoor might not have conferred any special advantage. Furthermore, the hereditary office occupied by Ælfric and his successors remained undefined in law until 1215, when the Magna Carta associated 'the service of rendering to us knives or arrows or the like' with the rank of 'petty serjeanty'.[12] To me this sounds like a demotion. Perhaps it was a stitch-up agreed by King John and his barons, as part of a top-down enforcement of the prevailing social order which reflected their disdain for their vassals. In any case, the hereditary service-holders of Shapley and Skerraton didn't have long to enjoy their status as petty serjeants, because in 1228 it was all forfeited to the crown.

Far more is known about the circumstances and the consequences of the 1228 forfeiture than we might reasonably expect, mainly because of the incredibly meticulous research undertaken by the Rev Oswald Reichel

---

10 [History of Buckfast Abbey] p.42. On pp.256-258 Hamilton dates the charter to c.1105. While in [New History of Buckfast Abbey] pp.37-38 Dom John Stephan argues for a later date, c.1148, this does not invalidate the idea that the name 'David' went with the office of 'royal huntsman'.

11 1 Samuel 16:21; 17:49; 20:41.

12 [Magna Carta] n.27.

in his translation and annotation of the Devonshire records in the Book of Fees, also known as the 'Testa Nevil'. This extraordinary resource is worth seeing – it cannot be 'read', in any conventional sense – if only to dispel any doubts about its accuracy and reliability.[13] For the present purpose of continuing to trace the origin of the Kingdons, however, it is sufficient to just pick out the bare bones of the key names, places, dates and events, as follows.

David of Shapley and Skerraton had three children: Roger Mirabel, Orresia, and Robert.[14] I have noted that within David's lifetime Orresia wed Walter and the happy couple set up home in the farm now known as Kendon. Subsequently it was claimed that this tenement had been given to Orresia as part of her marriage portion, but there is no trace of a written covenant to this effect, and it is likely that if David had been succeeded by his eldest son in the usual way then the estate would not have been divided. David was indeed succeeded by Roger Mirabel, but in 1228 Roger Mirabel was outlawed for murder and the entire service-holding was forfeited to the crown. Other than this outcome, nothing is known of the actual crime. We do not know who was murdered, or how, or why, or whether there had been a miscarriage of justice, or indeed whether there had been any crime at all. But from the severity of the punishment we can infer that the alleged victim belonged to the Norman elite, otherwise the whole affair could have been dismissed as yet another case of 'Englishry' and brushed under the carpet – or behind the tapestry, I should say.

In 1229 King Henry III gave the whole service-holding – that is, Shapley and Skerraton and the associated petty serjeanty – to Hubert de Burgh's personal physician, Walter the doctor.[15] Walter took possession of Skerraton, and of the farm now known as South Hookner, but when his bailiffs approached Kendon they found that its occupants were not for

---

13 See [Devon Book of Fees], in particular, for the 1228 forfeiture: pp.411-412; pp.423-424 n.1371 (including footnote 14); p.428 n.1452; pp.431-432 nn.1468-1472 (including footnote 26); p.441 nn.1503-1504; pp.452-453. On the same topic, a supplementary list of sources appears in [Devon Eyre 1238] p.97 n.595.

14 [Devon Surnames] p.89 suggests that David's wife may have been called Mirabel, hence Roger's unusual byname.

15 Walter the doctor was subsequently known as Walter de Skiredon (of Skerraton), Walter de Deveneys (of Devonshire), or Walter le Deveneys (the Devonshire man). In the court record reproduced in Figure 2 he is Walter le Deveneys.

moving. He resorted to litigation, and spent the rest of his life championing an increasingly ludicrous series of court cases, all to no avail. Orresia and family – now collectively 'of Kyngdon' – remained firmly ensconced in the rump of her ancestral homelands, and with the death of Walter the doctor in 1248 the matter ended. It may be that the only people to derive any benefit from this whole sorry tale are some latter-day scholars of jurisprudence, who regard the ancient and noble hereditary office of royal huntsman on Dartmoor as 'a rather interesting little serjeanty'.[16]

Reichel's last record of Kendon is dated 1274, when it was found to be held by Buckfast Abbey, by the gift of Nicholas de Kyngdon. At the same time Skerraton was found to be held by John de Boyvile and Dyonisia his wife, she being the daughter and heiress of Walter the doctor. And with these three new characters the story enters a whole new plane of reality, for the lurid allegations of their murderous property-war-cum-love-triangle and the subsequent spectral haunting of Buckfast Abbey have been told and retold sufficiently often that they have effectively passed into folklore. Both published histories of Buckfast Abbey, and both published histories of the Kingdon family, recount some or all of these claims, with varying degrees of credulity.[17] I prefer to focus on what is known from the historical record. Arranged chronologically, the relevant facts are as follows:

- When Walter the doctor died in 1248 he had no legitimate male heir, and Skerraton reverted to the crown by escheat. However, the king allowed Walter's widow Emma to retain custody of the land in trust for their daughters, then aged eight and five. With exaggerated caution Reichel hazards a rare 'conjecture', opining that such a concession was 'hardly likely … except in the case of a specially favoured subject.'[18]
- In 1257 Sir Stephen Bauzan died fighting the Welsh, and the following year his heir Richard Bauzan gave *totam terram meam de Holna*, 'all my lands of Holne', to the nearby Buckfast Abbey, 'for the souls of my father and my mother, and of my brother

16 [King's Serjeants] p.19.

17 [History of Buckfast Abbey] p.226; [New History of Buckfast Abbey] pp.90-95; [Kingdon Family] pp.8-9; [Kingdon Family Second Look] pp.16-19.

18 [Devon Book of Fees] pp.452-453.

Stephen Bauzan'.[19] But there is extant another undated charter in which Richard Bauzan gave *totam terram meam de Holne* to Nicholas de Kyngdon, in this case, in return for the service of a thirtieth part of a knight's fee, plus thirty shillings a year to Buckfast Abbey, 'for my soul and the soul of Stephen Bauzan'.[20] Hugh Watkin resolves this apparent contradiction by concluding that the latter gift 'probably refers to Holne Bozom as he had given his land in South Holne to Buckfast Abbey'.[21] The matching dedication to Stephen Bauzan suggests that the two charters were made around the same time, c.1258. If so then this is the earliest record that we have of Nicholas de Kyngdon.

- In 1264 Nicholas de Kyngdon witnessed a Buckfast Abbey charter.[22]
- In 1269 Nicholas de Kyngdon and John de Boyvile witnessed an agreement between Abbot Henry of Buckfast and Dionisia widow of Robert Burgh.[23] In that year Walter the doctor's eldest daughter would have been twenty-nine: certainly old enough to have wed, given birth to a couple of daughters, and been widowed. Was this the occasion that the newcomer John de Boyvile first met his future wife Dyonisia, in the presence of Nicholas de Kyngdon?
- In 1273 and on another unknown date Nicholas de Kyngdon and John de Boyvile witnessed two more Buckfast Abbey charters.[24]
- By 1274, as I have noted, Nicholas de Kyngdon had given Kendon to Buckfast Abbey, and John de Boyvile and Dyonisia his wife had set up home in Skerraton.
- In 1279 John de Boyvile and Dyonisia his wife lodged a plea alleging that she had been defrauded when still a minor. The court did not agree.[25]
- 'In the year 1280 Edward I appointed special Commissioners

19 [History of Buckfast Abbey] pp.90-96; [Cistercian Houses] pp.62-63; [Grandisson Register III] pp.1583-1585 nn.XXVII-XXX.

20 [Kingdon Family] pp.10-11; [Grandisson Register III] p.1603 n.LVII.

21 [History of Totnes 2] p.882.

22 [Grandisson Register III] p.1592 n.XL.

23 [123M/TB60].

24 [Grandisson Register III] pp.1577-1578 n.XIX; p.1556 n.II.

25 [Patent Rolls EdI 1272-1281] mem.27d p.406.

to make enquiry throughout the kingdom by what right the landholders held their estates, franchises, or other privileges.' 'David of Skeriton, no doubt a descendant of that David who figures in our earliest charter, held his land by the services of finding three arrows for the king's use, when he chose to hunt on Dartmoor. From David it passed to Roger de Mirabel, who had forfeited it for felony; and it had been re-granted to Walter, the king's physician, and had subsequently been alienated to Buckfast. It was contended by the Commissioners that the alienation without the royal consent was not legal, but nothing more seems to have been heard of the matter.'[26]

- The last reference to Nicholas de Kyngdon in the surviving records of Buckfast Abbey is dated 1284.[27]
- John de Boyvile and his direct descendants continued to hold Skerraton and South Hookner until at least 1417.[28]

Taken together, these historical facts contradict most of the details and erode much of the credibility of the chilling tale of 'Sir Nicholas de Kyngdon and the Ghost of Buckfast Abbey'.[29] In particular: Nicholas de Kyngdon was not a knight; nor was he a Norman; nor was he in possession of Kendon when John de Boyvile and Dyonisia his wife were living in Skerraton; nor did he murder either of them before they had a chance to raise a legitimate male heir; nor did he then suffer an early demise through receiving a minor wound from his own poisoned dagger.[30] On the contrary, judging by his long and constructive interaction with his neighbours, notably the gentle denizens of Buckfast Abbey but also including John de Boyvile himself, it is clear that Nicholas de Kyngdon was a pillar of rural Devon society in the thirteenth century, who did much to stabilise and rehabilitate his family's reputation and fortunes. And by 'his family' I mean, of course, the direct descendants of Ælfric of Shapley and Skerraton, for Nicholas de Kyngdon would not have been able to give Kendon to Buckfast Abbey if he had not been the legitimate male heir of

26 [History of Buckfast Abbey] p.107; p.114.

27 [New History of Buckfast Abbey] p.91.

28 [Stanborough 100 TN] pp.200-201.

29 This is the title of chapter 4 of [Kingdon Family Second Look].

30 There is no evidence refuting the existence of the ghost, however.

Walter de Kyngdon and Orresia his wife.

Little else is known of Nicholas de Kyngdon or his predecessors. We do not know why he gave Kendon to Buckfast Abbey, although with hindsight we may judge this to have been a wise deed, simultaneously making a clean break with the past and making new friends in high places. We do not know what happened to Walter de Kyngdon or Orresia his wife, although it is likely that they ended their days peacefully at home in Kendon, the first and last of that ilk. We do not know what happened to Orresia's younger brother Robert, although it is likely that he too ended his days on the smallholding near to Kendon that he'd acquired during the fragmentation of the family estate. And, finally, we do not know what happened to Roger Mirabel, although I imagine that being an outlaw would not have prevented him from accepting his sister's hospitality once in a while. Also he might have tried his luck in the local town, Totnes, where (again, I imagine) the pragmatic merchants might have been less bothered by his shady past than the feudal courts had been. In c.1282 a new member to the Totnes merchants guild received an intriguing endorsement, 'by right of Rogerus de Kyngdon', added to the margin of the Guild Roll.[31] Was this an elderly Roger Mirabel? Or maybe his son, or Orresia's? We may never know; but it is heartening to see that the family name still counted for something, despite the indelible stain of Roger Mirabel's alleged felony.

To recap: starting with Walter de Kyngdon and Orresia his wife, who in 1244 were the very first 'of Kyngdon', I have traced their lineage back to Orresia's ancestor Ælfric of Shapley and Skerraton in 1066-1086, and forward to their legitimate male heir Nicholas de Kyngdon in c.1258-1284. This last date is still 109 years before the birth of Roger Kyngdon of Trehunsey, who is seen as the common progenitor of the various West Country branches of the Kingdon family.[32] That's another four or five intermediate generations that we need to populate, but we don't have much to go on, because in this period only a small handful of apparently unrelated Kingdons are mentioned in the records. Nevertheless, by following the successful career path of just one of these Kingdons, it is possible to identify a narrow but continuous bloodline that miraculously survived the

31 [History of Totnes 1] p.87 n.290.

32 [Kingdon Family] pp.16-17; [Kingdon Family Second Look] pp.1-4. Trehunsey is in the parish of Quethiock in Cornwall; see map, Figure 1.

several cataclysms of the fourteenth century. It is my contention that the following records all refer to the same person, who, for the purpose of this narrative, I shall call 'John Kyngdon':

- Joh. de Kyndone received *primam tonsuram*, Totnes, 1311.[33]
- Joh. de Kyngdone was inducted as *accoliti*, Totnes, 1316.[34]
- Joh. de Kyngdone received *primam tonsuram*, Exeter, 1319.[35]
- Joh. de Kyngdone was inducted as *accoliti*, Exeter, 1321.[36]
- John de Kyngeston was appointed controller of the king's mine in the county of Devon, 1321.[37]
- Johannes de Kyngdon was parliamentary representative for Plympton, 1329-1330 and for a second time in 1330.[38]
- Johanne Kyndon witnessed a grant of land, Plympton, 1330.[39]
- John de Kyngdone of Plympton was the only Kingdon to be taxed in the Devon Lay Subsidy, 1332.[40]
- Johannes de Kyngdon was parliamentary representative for Plympton, 1339 and 1340.[41]
- Johannes Kyngdon was parliamentary representative for Plympton, 1341, 1348, 1350-1351, 1351-1352, and 1355.[42]

Let us examine each of these records in more detail.

Primam tonsuram was the first tonsure, or head-shaving, received by a novice on admission to a religious house. It signified that the recipient had been accepted for schooling in preparation for holy orders or for secular work. The fact that John Kyngdon received *primam tonsuram* twice suggests that he had a basic education at Totnes Priory followed

33 [Stapledon Register] p.486 n.XXXV; [Kingdon Family] p.9.

34 [Stapledon Register] p.509 n.LXXIII; also [Kingdon Family] p.9, where, copied from the same source, the name has been spelt 'John de Kingdone'.

35 [Stapledon Register] p.525 n.XCVII; [Kingdon Family] p.10.

36 [Stapledon Register] p.532 n.CXXII; [Kingdon Family] p.10.

37 [Fine Rolls III] mem.19 p.83; also [Kingdon Family] p.6, where, copied from the same source, the name has been spelt 'John de Kingesdun'.

38 [History of Plympton] p.178; [Kingdon Family] p.134.

39 [History of Plympton] p.209; also [Kingdon Family] p.13, where, copied from the same source, the name has been spelt 'Johanne Kyngdon'.

40 [Devon Lay Subsidy 1332] p.113.

41 [History of Plympton] p.178; [Kingdon Family] p.134.

42 [History of Plympton] pp.178-179; [Kingdon Family] p.134.

by a more advanced training at Exeter Cathedral. We cannot be sure of his age at either of these stages: although in principle the minimum age for *primam tonsuram* was fixed, in practice it was negotiable.[43] But if he was born in 1300 then he would have been eleven when commencing his basic education and nineteen when commencing his advanced training, which seems plausible enough. Even if this estimate is incorrect by a few years, it is clear that the age gap with Nicholas de Kyngdon (for example) is much too big for the latter to have been John's father. There must have been at least one intermediate generation.

Accoliti or acolyte was a minor order in the church, which did not prevent the holder from doing secular work or from getting married. Indeed, the absence of any record of John Kyngdon taking up holy orders indicates that he received an education in order to pursue a secular career. In those days this was a rare privilege, only open to those with money and influence. For this reason it is highly likely that John was a direct descendant of either Nicholas or Roger de Kyngdon, and the eventual heir of both. The only other record of a family member in this period announces the appointment of Adam de Kyngdone as Rector of Loxbeare in 1285.[44] As a priest Adam could not have been John's direct ancestor, but he could have been a great-uncle (for example). Loxbeare is near to Tiverton, where in the middle ages the castle was the principal seat of the powerful Earls of Devon. Once again this raises the prospect of Kingdon family members having access and influence in high places, with John Kyngdon being the principal beneficiary. Another unforeseen benefit of being schooled in a cloistered community was that he didn't starve during the Great Famine of 1315-1317.

In September 1321 John Kyngdon graduated as *accoliti* in Exeter, and three months later he was appointed controller of the king's mine in the county of Devon.[45] He was well-qualified for this office, being possessed of a good education, local knowledge, and a suitable family background. The

43 [Medieval Schools] chapter 8.

44 [Bronescombe Quivil Registers] p.348; [Kingdon Family] p.9.

45 This statement assumes a rare exception to my usual practice of not equating proper nouns ending 'don' and 'ton' (see Commentary, below). In this case I feel the exception is justified, as the resulting statement fits very nicely with the other pieces of evidence concerning John Kyngdon's career.

mine in question comprised a series of deep workings for the extraction of silver-bearing lead ore from a rich seam on the Bere Ferrers peninsula.[46] As controller John Kyngdon would have overseen the mine's operations and accounts. Additionally he may have supervised the regular coinages held at the stannary towns – Tavistock, Ashburton, and Chagford – which controlled the produce of the tin stream-workings on Dartmoor.[47] But he did not enjoy this position for long: by September 1322 another man, Simon Velde, had been named as controller in his place.[48] Nevertheless, I imagine that his tenure was sufficient for him to acquire the knowledge and the contacts to set up his own business, which (again, I imagine) probably involved the buying and selling of tin. My reason for this supposition is that in 1329 John Kyngdon was named as parliamentary representative for Plympton, which just the year before had been made a stannary town in place of Tavistock.[49] We do not know whether he was one of those who lobbied for this change, but it seems highly likely, given the circumstance of his subsequent elevation. Altogether, John Kyngdon represented Plympton at nine parliaments over twenty-seven years, including those held immediately before and after the Black Death of 1348-1349.

In terms of personal survival, John Kyngdon was a very lucky man, and a very rare one too. Not only did he survive the Great Famine and the Black Death, in 1332 he was the only Kingdon *in the whole of Devon* to be taxed. But there is a big difference between surviving and prospering. The plague 'almost ruined the stannaries', and the workings on Dartmoor never fully recovered.[50] So while John Kyngdon survived, his source of income did not, which harsh reality would have wiped out any intention to found a family dynasty in Plympton. To derive any lasting benefit from his established business, his heir would have been obliged to follow the inexorable drift of the tin mining industry towards the west – into

46 [Silver Mines] p.4; Peter Claughton, pers. comm.; Tom Greeves, pers. comm.

47 [Stannaries] p.45; pp.149-151.

48 [Close Rolls EdII 1318-1323] mem.25 p.598.

49 As [Stannary of Tavistock] makes clear, these two towns were great rivals at this time: Tavistock Abbey was the wealthiest religious house in Devon, and in return for payments to the king it held a sequence of profitable grants over both the Bere Ferrers mine and the Dartmoor stannaries; whilst Plympton's Priory came in a close second, and its ancient borough also had a feudal barony, held by the Earls of Devon.

50 [Stannaries] p.40.

Cornwall.[51] And the evidence suggests that this is precisely what happened.

As far as we can tell from the available records, the first Kingdon in Cornwall was William de Kyngdone, who received *primam tonsuram* at Boconnoc in October 1321.[52] This is all we know about William; nevertheless, it is of great significance. His family name is spelt the same as John's, as it appears in the same bishop's register only the month before. Doubtless they were brothers or first cousins. As for Boconnoc, this was not a religious house but a parish church that served the vast estate of the same name, which was just one of the properties of the foremost Cornish landholder of the age, Sir John Carminow.[53] In 1320 Carminow selected Boconnoc as his principal seat, whereupon the prospect of a rich living attracted to the parish an ambitious new Rector, Richard Lovecoke of Tiverton.[54] He was the son of Philip Lovecoke, who at that time was 'The most prominent Exeter importer … who was elected mayor ten times and was probably the richest man in Exeter.'[55] Such wealth and influence must have been an important factor in Richard's elevation to Boconnoc from his previous living in the quiet backwater of Manaton, on the east side of Dartmoor.[56] Furthermore, given his earlier proximity to their old stamping-grounds, Richard Lovecoke must have been acquainted with the Kingdon family well before he included William de Kyngdone in his first select group of just four novices. And it comes as no surprise that in John Kyngdon's 1316 *accoliti* batch there was a Henry Lovecoke, and in his 1319 *primam tonsuram* batch there was a Philip Lovecoke. Of course the families knew one another: that's how it worked.

Between the last record of John Kyngdon of Plympton and the birth of Roger Kyngdon of Trehunsey there is a gap of thirty-eight years, that is, two intermediate generations. There are records of three more members of the Kingdon family living in the West Country in this period, the second half of the fourteenth century. Firstly, John Kyngdone was inducted as

---

51 [Stannaries] pp.43-44.

52 [Stapledon Register] p.535 n.CXXVII; [Kingdon Family] p.10.

53 For an account of the Carminow family see [Extinct Cornish Families II]. Sir John Carminow also features in Daphne du Maurier's compelling re-imagining of the period, *The House on the Strand* (1969).

54 [Stapledon Register] p.191.

55 [Exeter Accounts] p.21.

56 [Stapledon Register] p.233.

tonsurati at a ceremony in Tiverton in 1370, and the following year John Kyngedone (surely the same person) was inducted as *acoliti* at a ceremony in Exeter.[57] Secondly, Walter Kyngdon was a juror in a legal inquisition at Launceston in 1392.[58] Thirdly, Richard Kingdon was a portreeve in Liskeard between 1394 and 1399.[59] We do not know whether any of these Kingdons were related. Nevertheless, it is instructive to include them in a simple generation table, as follows:[60]

b.c.1180	David (Shapley, Skerraton)
b.c.1210	Roger Mirabel (Shapley, Skerraton), Orresia (Kendon), Robert (Shapley)
b.c.1240	Nicholas de Kyngdon (Holne), Roger de Kyngdon (Totnes), Adam de Kyngdone (Loxbeare)
b.c.1270	?
b.c.1300	John Kyngdon (Plympton), William de Kyngdone (Boconnoc)
b.c.1330	John Kyng(e)done (Tiverton, Exeter)
b.c.1360	Walter Kyngdon (Launceston), Richard Kingdon (Liskeard)
b.1393	Roger Kyngdon (Trehunsey)

This table gives implausibly late birth dates for the generations of Roger Mirabel and Nicholas, and an implausibly early birth date for John Kyng(e)done, but the other dates fit quite nicely. The late birth dates could be corrected by assuming a shorter inter-generation timestep during the thirteenth century, and inserting another unknown generation before 1300. John Kyng(e)done's early birth date could be corrected with reference to the Black Death: perhaps he was a precious late-born son of John Kyngdon

57 [Brantyngham Register II] p.754 n.I; p.764 n.XVII. The spelling of '*acoliti*' is copied from the source.

58 [Launceston Cartulary] p.58 n.150; also [Kingdon Family] p.14 refers to the same hearing, but omits the names of the jurors, and instead mistakenly alters the name of one of the plaintiffs from 'Henrie Kyng' to 'Henrie Kyngdone'.

59 [History of Liskeard] p.256; [Kingdon Family] p.13.

60 The generation table is a useful tool for estimating the ages of family members. Typically, as here, it is anchored by a single known date, from which the corresponding dates of the other generations may be calculated, using a fixed timestep of thirty years.

of Plympton, his elder brothers all having perished in the plague. These amendable imperfections notwithstanding, this table indeed depicts the 'narrow but continuous bloodline' that connects the early inhabitants of Kendon on Dartmoor with Roger Kyngdon of Trehunsey in Cornwall. In addition it tracks each generation's discrete relocation as the family gradually migrated from Kendon to Trehunsey, and it monitors the evolution of the family name over this formative period.

The multiple natural and human disasters of the fourteenth century tested to destruction the feudal system. This did not bring about the equitable redistribution of the land, however. On the contrary, it meant that landholders effectively became landowners, which in turn meant that the rich could become even richer. If a landholder died without leaving a legitimate male heir then under feudalism the estate would escheat to the overlord, but with the breakdown of that system the local property magnates could descend and divide the spoils between them. In this viciously competitive environment, the chances of anyone acquiring their first little freeholding were remote. How, then, did the Kingdons acquire Trehunsey? As before, I suggest, the crucial factor was their access and influence in high places, that is, amongst people such as the Carminows, the Lovecokes, the Priors of Plympton, and, perhaps, the Earls of Devon. To use an ugly but apt colloquialism, these people were 'big beasts'. Now, even a big beast has to be careful not to bite off more than it can chew, and occasionally it is advantageous to allow the odd scrap to fall to a marginal scavenger, particularly if that scavenger might otherwise team up with another big beast. In any case, at some time in the fourteenth century Trehunsey fell to the Kingdons, and that's where Roger Kyngdon spent most or all his life, 1393-1471.

To recap: using official records rather than family hearsay, I have traced the Kingdon lineage from Ælfric of Shapley and Skerraton during the Norman Conquest all the way to Roger Kyngdon of Trehunsey four centuries later. The narrative is still not complete, however. As both published histories of the Kingdon family make clear, it has yet to be proved that Roger Kyngdon is 'the common progenitor of the various West Country branches of the Kingdon family'. In particular, there is a nasty little gap between 1515, when Roger's son Walter made his last will, and 1538-1540, when King Henry VIII's minister Thomas Cromwell mandated the keeping of parish registers and the Statute of Wills enabled landholders to name their inheritors. But we are in danger of using double standards here. From parish registers and property bequests it is relatively easy to determine who was the child of whom, because it is often explicitly stated; and it is from the reliability of such records that genealogists have derived their usual high standard of proof. Before 1538, however, these records did not exist, and it would be nonsensical to insist on the same level of rigour. Instead, as we have seen, we must rely on a variety of royal, ministerial, legal, ecclesiastical and municipal records, leavened with a general knowledge of English social history and analytical tools such as the generation table. It follows that we must also make do with a less exacting standard of proof, based on what can be substantiated 'beyond reasonable doubt'.[61] And if this more relaxed standard is deemed acceptable up to 1393, then it ought to be acceptable up to 1538. With this in mind, let us review the available evidence for this period.

Regarding Roger Kyngdon himself, we have three pieces of evidence. Firstly, in 1411 he did homage to Edmund Stafford Bishop of Exeter for lands in Lawhitton near to Launceston.[62] He was barely eighteen at the time, which suggests that this was his first foray into the business of agricultural landholding, perhaps in preparation for his eventual inheritance of Trehunsey. The fact that such a young man could acquire a landholding in this way is another indication of the enduring influence of the Kingdon name amongst people in high places. Secondly, in 1437 Roger testified at a legal inquisition in Launceston, in proceedings that are of little interest in themselves, except that they enable us to calculate his birth date.[63] Thirdly, there is the monumental brass commemorating Rogerus Kyngdon and Johanna his wife in St Hugh's church, Quethiock, which as a result is regarded as 'the family shrine'.[64] Apart from its antiquity, the most striking feature of this brass is its depiction of the couple's eleven sons and five daughters: surely a proud display of true wealth and success, given the ghastly events of the previous century.

61 What constitutes this 'less exacting standard of proof' is discussed in the Commentary, below.

62 [Stafford Register Index] p.231; [Kingdon Family] p.10; p.16.

63 [Blanchminster's Charity]; [Kingdon Family] p.16.

64 [Brasses of Cornwall] pp.19-20; [Kingdon Family] p.17; [Kingdon Family Second Look] p.1; pp.8-13; p.15.

Regarding the offspring of Rogerus Kyngdon and Johanna his wife (henceforth 'Roger and Johanna'), our main source of information is the will of their son, Walter.[65] This important document has been analysed in depth by the authors of the two published histories of the Kingdon family, F B Kingdon (FBK) and A S Kingdon (ASK).[66] Rather than reiterating and then dissecting all of their interesting and important points of agreement and disagreement, I will simply add in my ha'penny's-worth, as follows:

- In my opinion, ASK is right to question FBK's assumption that Walter was the eldest son of Roger and Johanna. That is, I agree with the view that Walter is depicted at the upper end of his line of brothers not because he was the eldest but because of his rank in the church. Indeed, for the same reason, it probably fell to Walter to commission and pay for the brass, in which case he might have been more concerned with his own glorification than with the commemoration of his parents. Furthermore, by the pre-1540 rule of primogeniture only the eldest son could inherit a family estate and with it the right and duty to have a legitimate male heir of his own; thus it would make no sense to encourage or allow him to become a priest. Only younger sons could follow a religious calling.
- ASK is also correct when he amends FBK's tentative transcription of 'Edward Kyngdon at (sea?)' to 'Edward Kyngdon at Fene' or 'Edward Kyngdon at Venn'. But his suggestion that this might refer to Venn House in Lamerton near Tavistock is unfounded. Given the brevity of the address, Venn must have been much closer to the family homestead in Quethiock than Lamerton, a dozen miles away and in a different county. And indeed there is an old farm of precisely that name which is directly adjacent to Trehunsey. Their farm buildings are in sight of one another and less than six hundred yards apart.
- Three people called Walter Kyngdon feature in the will: the testator; the testator's godson; and the Vicar of Lamerton. FBK tentatively equates the latter two, but this is unfounded. Indeed, I can think of several good reasons why they should not be equated.

65 [Cornish Wills] pp.158-159.

66 [Kingdon Family] pp.20-23; [Kingdon Family Second Look] pp.88-90.

Firstly, the will is written in a plain and matter-of-fact style that avoids the use of synonyms. Secondly, the testator's godson was also his great-nephew, and when the will was written he was probably too young to have been an ordained priest. Thirdly, the two main beneficiaries of the will were the testator's godson and Edward Kyngdon at Venn, while the two executors were the Vicar of Lamerton and Edward Kyngdon again. If the testator's godson were the Vicar of Lamerton then the main beneficiaries would have been the executors, with no independent third party: which surely would have been a recipe for disaster.

- According to ASK, 'What does appear certain is that the large family of Roger and Johanna did not cause such a population explosion as might have been thought. While one or two sons might have remained bachelors, it would seem from Walter's will that only three had children and that apart from Walter, a celibate priest, there is no record of any other reaching manhood. This would also squash any theory that unknown brothers of Walter might have established colonies of Kingdons where on present knowledge, we are uncertain of the origins.' This is unfounded. In those days, after the decline of feudalism but before the advent of parish registers and property bequests, it would have been quite usual for fortune-seeking young men to migrate unnoticed, as they sought more attractive terms for their skills and labour. The unnamed sons of Roger and Johanna had no prospects at home, so why wouldn't they just up and leave? And if they did go further afield – to the rich farming lands of North or Mid Devon, for instance – then there is no reason to suppose that they would remain in touch with the folks back home. Even if they could read and write, there was no uniform postal service by which they could send letters to one another. Walter's omission of his unnamed brothers from his will might have been because he simply did not know where they were or what they were doing. That is, I suspect it was a result of poor communication rather than malice or, even less likely, some mysterious 'unnamed brother death syndrome'.

With these points in mind, I have revised FBK's 'Pedigree Chart of Trehunsey Kingdons' in a transposed generation table, as follows:[67]

b.1393	**b.c.1420**	**b.c.1450**	**b.c.1480**
Roger Kyngdon m. Johanna (Trehunsey)			
	s.1 John Kyngdon		
		s.1.1 John Kyngdon (Trehunsey)	
		da.1.1 Margery Kyngdon m. John Manaton (Kilworthy)	
	s.2 Edward Kyngdon, Yeoman of the Crown (Westminster)		
		s.2.1 Edward Kyngdon (Venn)	
	s.3 William Kyngdon (St Cleer)		
		s.3.1 John Kyngdon (Looe)	
			s.3.1.1 Walter Kyngdon (s.4's godson)
		s.3.2 Edward Kyngdon m. Juliana Monke?	
		da.3.1 Margaret Kyngdon m.1 John Borlase m.2 Thomas Tregian	
		da.3.2 Joan Kyngdon m. Thomas Langlion	
		da.3.3 Agnes Kyngdon m. Maynard	
	s.4 Walter Kyngdon, Canon and Prebendary of Swords (Looe, St Cleer)		
	s.5		
	s.6		
	s.7		
	s.8		
	s.9		
	s.10		
	s.11		
	da.1		
	da.2		
	da.3		
	da.4		
	da.5		

67 By swapping rows and columns, the transposed generation table enables the depiction of parent-child relationships. Thus it can reproduce all the information that is portrayed in a pedigree chart (family tree), while happily dispensing with the need to have any sense of composition or skill in design.

A few comments are in order:

- This format compels us to acknowledge the existence of all the unnamed children of Roger and Johanna, and emphasises the absurdity of ASK's suggestion that sons 5-11 all died off with not one legitimate male heir between them.
- Even if Johanna were perpetually pregnant, it would still take her a dozen years to have sixteen children. Clearly, 'b.c.1420' and subsequent dates are only very rough estimates.
- The named sons of Roger and Johanna have been listed in the age order suggested by ASK.
- The family of Kilworthy, variously known as Manaton, Mannaton, Mananton or Manington, derived their name from a hamlet in South Hill (near Callington, midway between Tavistock and Liskeard), which 'is not to be confused with the East Dartmoor parish of Manaton.'[68]
- Roger and Johanna's son Edward had a distinguished career as a Yeoman of the Crown, that is, 'a servant or attendant in a royal or noble household, usually of a superior grade, ranking between a sergeant and a groom, or between a squire and a page.'[69] To me this sounds very much like the rank of petty serjeant held by Edward's ancestors. It is a sobering thought that it took over two centuries of unceasing endeavour by a relatively privileged family for just one of their number to experience the status that had once been theirs by birthright.
- Roger and Johanna's son William was parliamentary representative for Liskeard in 1452-1453.[70] Liskeard was a stannary town, and William lived in the parish of St Cleer, where even today the landscape is dominated by the scars of many centuries of mining activity. Perhaps he followed the example of his ancestor John Kyngdon of Plympton and worked in the tin trade?

---

68 [Coat of Arms at Kilworthy] p.322. Kilworthy is near to Tavistock.

69 [Kingdon Family] p.26.

70 [History of Liskeard] p.309; [Kingdon Family] p.134. In 1467 William's brother Edward also represented Liskeard at parliament, see [History of Liskeard] p.292; [Kingdon Family] p.134.

- It is known that Juliana Monke married Edward Kyngdon, but it is not known whether this Edward was the son of William Kyngdon (as shown) or his cousin at Venn.
- Roger and Johanna's son Walter had a distinguished career in the church. Indeed, almost lost amongst his list of ecclesiastical honours is the fact that he was Vicar of St Cleer from 1465 to 1497. St Cleer is less than five miles from Quethiock. It is increasingly evident that any account of the early history of the Kingdons in Cornwall would be incomplete if it merely focused on their tenure of Trehunsey and on 'the family shrine' of St Hugh's.
- Roger and Johanna's son 'M. Kyngdon' was included by FBK on the basis of a solitary entry in the Exeter College Register. A more careful inspection of this entry indicates that in fact it refers to Walter Kyngdon, that is, 'M.' is an abbreviation for 'Master'.[71]

The most striking aspect of Walter Kyngdon's will is the manifest geographical and fraternal closeness of the families of the elder sons of Roger and Johanna. Trehunsey and Venn are next to one another; St Cleer is five miles to the northwest; and Looe is ten miles to the south. Walter's two main beneficiaries were descended from his brothers Edward and William, and if they had both predeceased him then the son of his brother John would have inherited in their place.[72] In 1515, at least, the 'folks back home' operated very much as an extended family. Accordingly, it really doesn't matter whether the Kingdon bloodline continued through John, or Edward, or William. All that we need to show is that the bloodline *did* continue, by constructing a generation table similar to that which connects the early inhabitants of Kendon with Roger Kyngdon of Trehunsey. Indeed, although we are handicapped by the paucity of primary resources of the calibre of Walter's will, there are several other pieces of evidence which support just such a construction, as follows.

71 [Kingdon Family] p.28; [Exeter College Register] p.42.

72 Walter's 'two main beneficiaries', his godson Walter Kyngdon and Edward Kyngdon at Venn, each received landholdings in Looe. Presumably as a priest Walter was exempt from the usual rule of primogeniture, and he could bequeath his land to whomsoever he chose.

'The last male representative of the Kyngdons at Trehunsey was Thomas Kyngdon, who was dead before the year 1557.'[73] It appears that Thomas Kyngdon neither had a legitimate male heir nor did he write a will, because in that year his sister's daughters' husbands successfully claimed his estate and carved it up between them. Robert Trencreek and Anne his wife took 'the moiety of nine messuages, nine gardens, one hundred acres of land, forty acres of meadow, one hundred acres of pasture, six acres of wood, and sixty acres of furze and heath in Kyngdon, Overramannaton, Lovecott, Overrahampton, Knotham, Cowlstyck, Penhole, Pennacadyck, Tringale and Trewynt', while Henry Chiverton and Alice his wife took 'the moeity of three messuages, six gardens, one cottage, two corn mills, one forge, one dovecote, one hundred acres of land, twenty acres of meadow, one hundred acres of pasture, ten acres of wood, and forty acres of furze and heath in Treunsey, *alias* Trehunsey, Treunsey Milles, Trehunsey Cote, and Quethiock'. Although some of these places defy identification, it appears that none of Trencreek's portion was in the parish of Quethiock, and none of Chiverton's portion was outside the same parish. Furthermore, it appears that none of Trencreek's several little parcels of land were in the parishes of St Cleer or East Looe, while Chiverton's portion in Quethiock did not include Venn. Thus Thomas Kyngdon was the heir of the Kingdons of Trehunsey, but he was not the heir of any of the descendants of the younger sons of Roger and Johanna. Assuming that Thomas was in his seventies when he died, we obtain the following revision to FBK's 'Table Showing the Passing of Trehunsey':[74]

---

73 [Brasses of Cornwall] p.19.

74 [Kingdon Family] p.30. My table is quite different from FBK's because it takes account of the later discovery that Joan, wife of William Vivian and heiress of Trehunsey, was the sister and not the daughter of Thomas Kyngdon.
See [Chiverton Book of Obits V] p.280, which amends the information in FBK's reference, [Brasses of Cornwall] pp.19-20; pp.57-58; pp.73-75 (which in turn comes from [Survey of Cornwall] and [Visitation of Cornwall]).

b.c.1450	**b.c.1480**	**b.c.1510**	**b.c.1540**	**b.c.1570**	**b.c.1600**
s.1.1 John Kyngdon (Trehunsey)					
	Thomas Kyngdon (Trehunsey)				
		No surviving male issue			
	Joan Kyngdon m. William Vivian				
		Anne/Anis Vivian m. Robert Trencreek (St Erme)			
			Katherine Trencreek m. Digory Polwhele		
				Isabel Polwhele m. Richard Chiverton	
		Alice Vivian m. Henry Chiverton (Trehunsey)			
			Richard Chiverton m. Isabel Polwhele		
				Henry Chiverton m. Emlin Buller	
					Sir Richard Chiverton

The acquisition continued. Somehow, by the time he died in 1617, Richard Chiverton (who married his cousin's daughter, Isabel Polwhele) held several more properties in Quethiock, including Venn.[75] But 'it came wi' a lass, it'll gang wi' a lass': Sir Richard Chiverton (who was Lord Mayor of London in 1658) had no sons, and on his death his various landholdings, including Trehunsey and Venn, were subsumed into the vast estate of his daughter's husband, Sir John Coryton.[76] The 'Passing of Trehunsey' is a perfect example of my earlier point about the rich getting richer.

The Kingdons of St Cleer were more tenacious than those of Quethiock. William Kyngdon lived in the hamlet now known as Trenouth, and he had a son who lived at a nearby farm now known as Newton.[77] Between these places there are two more farms called Lower and Higher Trethake, and next to the latter is another farm called Higher Tretharrup. In St Cleer churchyard, beside the path at the point where one can turn off to enter the church, there are gravestones commemorating four of the daughters of

75 [Brasses of Cornwall] p.74.

76 Trehunsey and Venn remained part of the Coryton Estate until 1919, when their holdings in Quethiock (which by then comprised most of the parish) were auctioned piecemeal.

77 It is likely that 'Newton' is a modern contraction of 'New-town' or 'New-land'. In [Kingdon Family] p.28 FBK writes it as 'Newlyn', which is a fishing town near to Penzance, in the far west of the county. Similarly, in his error-strewn transcription of the 1392 legal inquisition at Launceston (see above), FBK interprets 'Newelond' as 'Newlyn'. He is surely mistaken in both cases.

'Richard and Mary Kingdon late of Trethake and Tretharrup', the longest-lived being Anne, who died in 1892 aged eighty-four. ASK has traced the St Cleer family tree back from Anne and her sisters to 'Samuell Kingdome d?1700'.[78] While this still leaves a substantial gap, there can be no doubt that this is the same family, living in the same region of the same parish for over four hundred years. But it appears that Anne was the last of her line.

At the bottom of his 'Pedigree Chart of Trehunsey Kingdons' FBK has appended 'b. circ. 1540 John Kingdon, of Coldridge.' John is the progenitor of the Coldridge and Holsworthy branches of the Kingdon family.[79] On arrival in the parish of Coldridge in 1563 he took up residence in East Leigh. 'The Kingdons owned at one time practically all the hamlet of East Leigh and the house is supposed to have been given to John Kingdon by a relative in Cornwall.'[80] Who was John's benefactor? Not any Kingdon of Trehunsey: Thomas, the last of that line, had died by 1557, and all of his fixed assets had been claimed by the Trencreeks and the Chivertons. Not any Kingdon of St Cleer: all of their resources would have been used to sustain their own small but viable branch of the family. Of all the descendants of Roger and Johanna identified in Walter Kyngdon's will, this only leaves Edward Kyngdon at Venn. Did he have descendants? Possibly. Did one of those descendants sell Venn to the Chivertons? Possibly. And did the proceeds of this sale go towards John Kingdon's acquisition of East Leigh? Possibly. Put it this way: we don't know of any other family member who had that kind of money at the time. So here is the promised generation table:

78 [Kingdon Family Second Look] p.98.

79 [Kingdon Family] pp.146-159 Charts I-VIII. John Kingdon may also be the progenitor of the Thorverton branch, see [Kingdon Family] pp.160-166 Charts IX-XII. Thorverton is midway between Tiverton and Exeter.

80 [Kingdon Family] p.71. Unlike Kendon, which was rebuilt in 1675, and Trehunsey, where the present farmhouse was built by the Coryton Estate, East Leigh remains intact, albeit sympathetically restored and tastefully refurbished.

b.c.1180	David (Shapley, Skerraton)
b.c.1210	Roger Mirabel (Shapley, Skerraton), Orresia (Kendon), Robert (Shapley)
b.c.1240	Nicholas de Kyngdon (Holne), Roger de Kyngdon (Totnes), Adam de Kyngdone (Loxbeare)
b.c.1270	?
b.c.1300	John Kyngdon (Plympton), William de Kyngdone (Boconnoc)
b.c.1330	John Kyng(e)done (Tiverton, Exeter)
b.c.1360	Walter Kyngdon (Launceston), Richard Kingdon (Liskeard)
b.1393	Roger Kyngdon (Trehunsey)
b.c.1420	s.2 Edward Kyngdon, Yeoman of the Crown (Westminster)
b.c.1450	s.2.1 Edward Kyngdon (Venn)
b.c.1480	?
b.c.1510	?
b.c.1540	John Kingdon (Coldridge)

John Kingdon's claim of descent from Roger and Johanna is quite weak, being based on family hearsay rather than documentary evidence. But even weaker are the claims of the other West Country branches of the Kingdon family, at Launceston, North Molton, South Molton, and Exeter, which simply refer to their use of the same name and the same coat of arms.[81] This doesn't mean that they *weren't* descended from Roger and Johanna; for, with that number of sons roaming around the countryside, who else could have been responsible for the subsequent proliferation of Kingdons?[82] All the same, as my history teacher used to write, 'Could do better.' And on that downbeat note, I conclude this description of the origin of the Kingdons.

81 See, for example, [Kingdon Family] p.16: 'The Launceston, North and South Molton, Coldridge and Exeter Kingdons all used the same coat of arms, showing a common ancestry.'

82 Many of these Kingdons were in North Molton, see [Kingdon Family Second Look] pp.20-22. On p.21 ASK wonders whether John Kingdon of Coldridge was the 'John, sonne of John Kyngdon' who was baptised in North Molton in 1540. In this scenario, however, it is difficult to see why a relative in Cornwall would choose to be so generous to John Kingdon of Coldridge, and not to any other family member in or from North Molton.

Middleword

Some readers may be feeling rather cheated by this rather abrupt and negative ending to what otherwise has been 'quite a story'. After all, what I had claimed to be 'unequivocal' has, in the end, turned out to be problematic and constrained. The truth is, in order to write this narrative I have had to play a little trick on everyone – myself included. Throughout, in order to empathise with the various family members and to understand their situations, I have maintained the belief that they are significant and meaningful to me and to others. To that end, I have tried to imagine that I am addressing the living descendants of Roger Kyngdon of Trehunsey – while knowing full well that this is a group of people whose existence has yet to be proved. Whilst useful and productive, this doublethink is also quite taxing, intellectually and emotionally. Seeking reassurance, I have written up the main aspects of the underlying research, as follows.

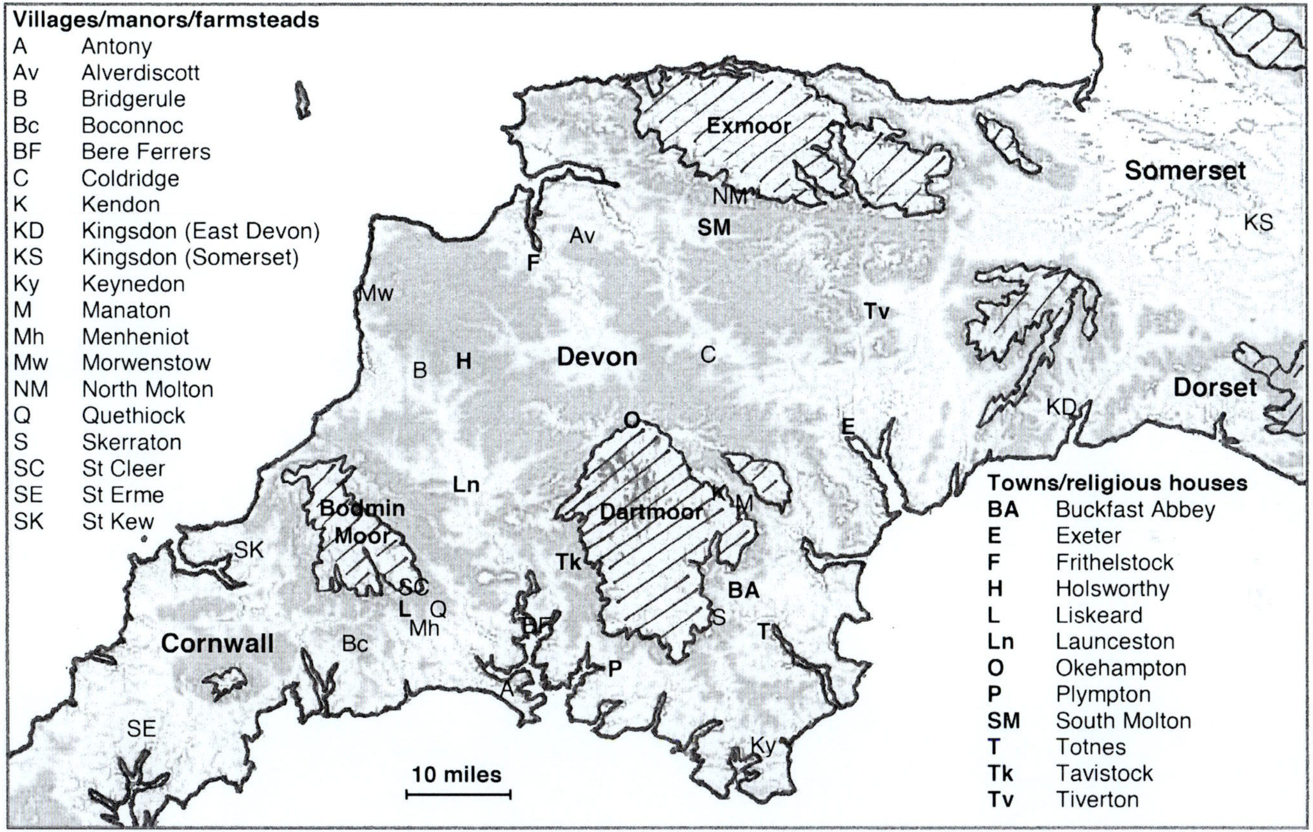

Figure 1 A map of South West England locating some of the places mentioned in the text.

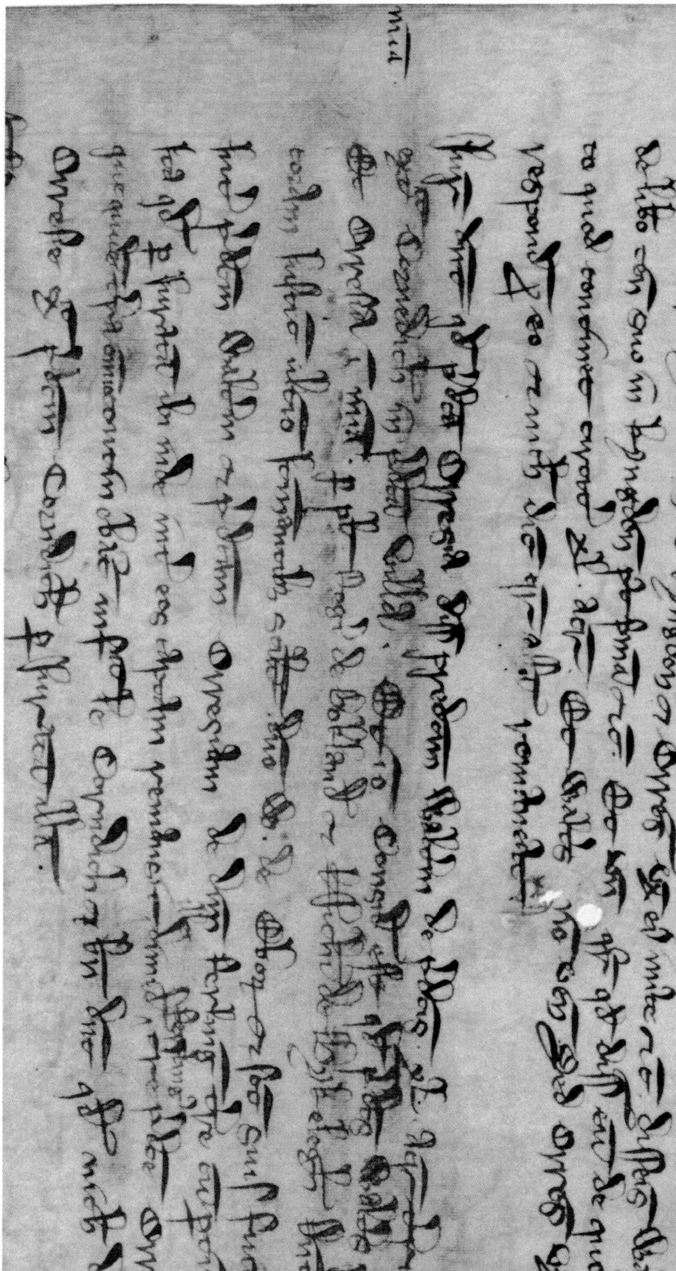

Figure 2 Plea by Walter de Kyngdon and Orresia his wife at the Devon eyre of 1244.
Detail from [JUST 1/175] mem.9, electronic scan courtesy The National Archives of the UK.

Commentary

The preceding narrative is predicated on the hypothesis that the Kingdons originated from Kendon on Dartmoor. It didn't take a great flash of inspiration to come up with this idea; just a healthy imagination, a general knowledge of English social history, and a practical awareness of the contents of the published histories of the Kingdon family. Subsequently, given this idea, it wasn't difficult to unearth a quantity of evidence which could then be used to support and shape the resulting story. For this task the main requirements were plenty of time and persistence, and easy access to the internet and the local archives.[83] But, in this case, what's to stop the end product from being a mere 'just-so story'? In what way has it been substantiated 'beyond reasonable doubt'? For that matter, what does this legal phrase mean, when used in the current non-legal context?

I am not a lawyer, nor am I a trained historian. I am a scientist, and my present use of the phrase 'beyond reasonable doubt' derives more from my understanding of scientific method than it does from the norms and procedures of any other field. To me this phrase means the following: firstly, that there is a well-defined 'preferred hypothesis', that is, a simple true-or-false proposition which can be made the basis of a coherent explanation of subsequent observed events; secondly, that this preferred hypothesis is supported by the available evidence to the extent that a reasonable person would have no difficulty in accepting the associated reconstruction of events; and, thirdly, that there is no other hypothesis which is supported by the available evidence, as judged by the same reasonable person using the same criterion. In our case, the first and second points are covered by the preceding narrative. Now it is necessary to address the third point, that is,

83 [DHC]; [CRO].

to take a close look at the possible alternatives to the idea that the Kingdons originated from Kendon on Dartmoor. This is best done through inquisition, that is, by posing a number of specific, closed questions, each of which examines a small but significant aspect of this preferred hypothesis and the subsequent narrative. These are the principal questions that I asked – and answered, to my satisfaction – prior to committing to a single view:

- How did the Kingdons get their name?
- Where was Kingdon?
- How did the Kingdons survive and prosper in feudal society?
- Who held Trehunsey before the Kingdons?
- Choughs or magpies?

In the following I summarise my answers to each of these questions in turn.

How did the Kingdons get their name?

I have noted that the name 'Kingdon' is derived from the Old English (OE) words for 'king' and 'hill'. This, at least, is not disputed; indeed, it is prominent amongst FBK's opening observations.[84] But one of his references, *A Glossary of Cornish Names*, then proceeds to confuse matters by interpreting 'Kingdon' as 'the king's hill', and equating it with 'Kingston'.[85] No: the possessive 's' is rarely found in the middle of the name, and there is a big difference between the endings 'don' and 'ton'. Specifically, in OE the suffix 'don' means 'hill' or 'down', while 'ton' or 'town' means 'enclosure' or 'homestead'. To see why this matters, consider the number of times these words and their variants occur in the *Calendar of the Patent Rolls*:[86]

84 [Kingdon Family] p.1.

85 [Glossary of Cornish Names] p.78.

86 [Patent Rolls Search]. No great significance should be attached to my searching for these terms in the Patent Rolls rather than any other court record such as the Fine Rolls. My reason for using this particular search facility is entirely pragmatic, that is, 'because it's there'.

Search term	Count	Search term	Count
Kyngeston Kingeston	1419 93	Kyngesdon Kingesdon	40 2
Kyngston Kingston	9 591	Kyngsdon Kingsdon	0 8
Kyngeton Kingeton	11 0	Kyngedon Kingedon	0 0
Kyngton Kington	128 8	Kyngdon Kingdon	0 0

These statistics show very clearly that in medieval times the Kingdon family name was highly distinctive and unusual. Of course, it's possible that on the few occasions he heard 'Kingdon' a medieval court clerk might have unthinkingly substituted the 'd' sound with a 't' sound and written some variant of 'Kyngeston'. And it's possible that on the few occasions he read the Kingdon family name a subsequent transcriber might have altered it to some variant of 'Kyngeston', again, with little further thought other than irritation at the apparent inconsistencies in the text. But in both cases these errors would have arisen only because of the relative unfamiliarity of the Kingdon family name; which again underlines its distinctiveness.

The rarity of the Kingdon family name can be put to good use. In particular, when searching for it in old documents I've *usually* been able to ignore the much more common variants having the suffix 'ton'. I've inserted 'usually' because there may well be some instances where the medieval court clerk or a subsequent transcriber has got it wrong; as I suspect is the case for the 1321 record of the appointment of John de Kyngeston as controller of the king's mine in the county of Devon. But, as in that case, such exceptions can only be justified if there is already a preponderance of evidence in favour of a different interpretation.

Regarding the spelling of the name, FBK lists the main variants as they appear in the old records, while ASK focuses on the more recent adaptations.[87] My view is that one cannot learn anything from an old

87 [Kingdon Family] pp.1-2; [Kingdon Family Second Look] pp.5-6; pp.56-59; pp.62-63; p.128.

document – Figure 2, for example – unless one develops a very relaxed attitude towards orthography and similar minutiae. The significance and reliability of a particular piece of evidence is determined by its consistency with other pieces of evidence, rather than by its consistency with arbitrary spelling norms. This appears to be the approach taken by Reichel for his analysis of the Devon Book of Fees, which I take to be the absolute gold standard in this field. As for how *we* spell *our* names: well, I spell mine 'Kingdon' because that's how it's spelt on my birth certificate; other criteria are available.

If – as I assert – the proper noun 'Kingdon' is OE, then the medieval Kingdons were English, that is, Anglo-Saxons. And if they were English then they were not Cornish, or Welsh, or Irish, or Britons, or Vikings, or Normans, or Bretons, or French. It is an interesting exercise to try to work out the family's name if in medieval times they had been known for living on a hypothetical hill in West Cornwall that was formerly associated with an unnamed king. My best guess is 'Brynrig', from the Common Brittonic words for 'hill' ('bryn') and 'king' ('ri' or 'rig'), which over time might be rendered as 'Brownrigg'. In any case it is completely unlike 'Kingdon'. Another exercise is to look for some variant of the Kingdon family name in the lists of knights who are supposed to have accompanied William the Conqueror in 1066. It is conspicuous by its absence.

If – as I assert – the medieval Kingdons were English, then they didn't live in West Cornwall. They might have lived in the southeast of the county, but only if they'd migrated there from further east, that is, from Devon. Furthermore, since all the early instances of the name include the preposition 'de' – 'of Kingdon' – then we should be looking for the place of the same name.[88] And that leads directly on to the next research question.

88 The implicit assumption here is that the Kingdon family name is locative, that is, it refers to a specific place. This is consistent with evidence in [Devon Surnames] which suggests that the majority of Devon family names that became hereditary in the medieval period were locative.

Where was Kingdon?

This is the heading of a short paragraph which appears on the penultimate page of the final supplement of ASK's history of the Kingdon family.[89] It is a pity that he has left it so late to ask this excellent question, and that he hasn't exerted himself to answer it. The paragraph commences, 'In all the research we have made we seem never to have come across any reference to Kingdon as a place name.' Clearly by this point ASK has forgotten that near the beginning of his book he has referred to 'the blood-thirsty knight' Nicholas de Kyngdon 'going back to die from the effects of his poisoned wound in his own house of Kingdon (Kendon).'[90] However, ASK is not alone in overlooking evidence the importance of which may be obvious only with the benefit of hindsight. FBK likewise discovers and then neglects a direct reference to Kendon, in a deed recording its sale to Henry Denys following the Dissolution of the Monasteries.[91] But that's enough about Kendon, which has been discussed at considerable length already. Instead, in reviving ASK's question I intend to explore where *else* was Kingdon – with the hope that I can find reasons to eliminate most or all of these alternatives from my enquiries – as follows.

- Higher Kingdon and Lower Kingdon, Alverdiscott, Devon. From their names, their location, and their rarity, it is natural to assume that one or both of these dwellings once comprised an original Kingdon family homestead. But caution is required, for several reasons. Firstly, on the 1809 Ordnance Survey First Series map of Mid Devon these places are called 'Kingdoms' and 'Lower Kingdoms' respectively, which use of the possessive 's' suggests that they were named after their occupants, rather than the other way round.[92] Secondly, whilst places called 'Kingdon' are rare

89 [Kingdon Family Second Look] p.129.

90 [Kingdon Family Second Look] p.17, which in turn quotes verbatim from [New History of Buckfast Abbey] p.93 (with appropriate attribution).

91 [Kingdon Family] p.31. Interestingly, this 1542 deed refers to Kendon being in the tenure of 'John Nawseworthye alias Kyndon' prior to its sale. The Nosworthy family clearly had an affinity for the place, because they were back in residence by c.1600 and remained there for several generations until c.1739. Also they would have been responsible for the rebuilding of the farmhouse in 1675.

92 The map might be wrong, however. After all, the map of Dartmoor in the same 1809 Ordnance Survey First Series refers to Kendon as 'Skinnings'!

now, this might not have been the case *previously*, so we must guard against the tendency to unthinkingly associate each newly-discovered instance with the one region that we know about. Thirdly, although the old records contain numerous references to places called 'Kingdon' in this locality, none of these eliminate ambiguity by also referring to the parish of Alverdiscott.[93] Fourthly, people make mistakes.[94] And, finally, neither published history of the Kingdons associates any branch of the family with Higher Kingdon or Lower Kingdon. *Retain – with reservations.*

- Keynedon, South Devon. FBK quotes old records in which this place is called 'Kenedon' or 'Kynedon'.[95] However, 'Keynedon (pronounced 'Kennedon') is an Old-English name, meaning the hill of Coena's people.'[96] *Reject.*
- Kingdon Farm, Antony, Cornwall. This might be the 'Kyngdon' taken by Robert Trencreek and Anne his wife in the 1557 division of the estate of Thomas Kyngdon of Trehunsey. (There are no other obvious candidates in East Cornwall.) The farm is on the Rame peninsula, which is very picturesque, but there are no local landmarks or topographical features that would explain why it has been called 'Kingdon'. Thus it is likely that it was named after its occupants, rather than the other way round. *Reject.*
- Kingsdon, East Devon. This is the site of a former manor house which is close to Colyton. Although it is not mentioned in either of the Kingdon family histories, ASK misses it by a mere whisker when he discusses 'The Kingdons of Colyton'; and also, in a completely different context, when he speculates that there might be some kind of link between the Kingdons and the Courtenays

93 See, for example, [CP 25/1/44/64] n.67; [Fine Rolls IX] mem.34 pp.308-309; [Chittlehampton] n.1.

94 For example, [Kingdon Family] p.3 refers to Joan Copleston marrying 'Henry Kingdon of Kingdon, Alverdiscot', but this is contradicted by family trees downloaded from [Copleston], which show that in 1608 *Elizabeth* Copleston married Henry Kingdon of *Saltash*, and that they had no direct association with Kingdon in *Alverdiscott*, which was the home of Elizabeth's cousin, Christopher Copleston (1564-1637).

95 [Kingdon Family] pp.4-5.

96 [Keynedon Barton] p.128.

(that is, the family of the Earls of Devon, who by chance also held land in the vicinity of Colyton).[97] There is no evidence of any such link, however. Furthermore, in the 1392 *Inquisitions Post Mortem* of Margaret de Courtenay, and in Bishop Brantyngham's register, the name of the manor is given as 'Kyngestone'.[98] That is, originally it was spelt with a 't' and not a 'd'. *Reject.*

- Kingsdon Manor, Kingsdon, Somerset. In medieval times Somerset was a relatively populous and prosperous county, quite separate and distinct from Devon and Cornwall. There was little incentive for its inhabitants to migrate west, and there is little evidence that they did. *Reject.*
- Kingston Manor, Isle of Wight. It is likely that this was the home of John de Kingesdon who in 1351-1355 acted as bailiff, clerk and guardian for the island.[99] The Earls of Devon held Wight until 1293, but this is not particularly remarkable, as they held many lands at that time. There is no evidence that the inhabitants of Kingston Manor ever migrated to the West Country. The 't' in the name raises further doubts.[100] *Reject.*
- Kyngdon Manor, Deanery of Hartland, Devon. There is documentary evidence that this was owned by Frithelstock Priory, and for this reason it cannot be dismissed so easily, even though its location remains a mystery.[101] Furthermore, before 1066 the Saxon kings held several valuable estates in North Devon, and therefore we have to allow for the possibility that any number of

97 [Kingdon Family Second Look] p.91; pp.118-120; p.124.

98 [IPM Margaret de Courtenay]; [Brantyngham Register I] p.455.

99 [Kingdon Family] p.7.

100 Although in all the records John de Kingesdon's name is spelt with a 'd', this appears to have been a matter of clerical convention, because in at least one index the entry reads, 'Kyngesdon, Kyngeston, John de, king's clerk'. See [Fine Rolls VI] p.536.

101 [Frithelstock Priory] p.170; [Kingdon Family] pp.3-4. In these references Higher Kingdon and Lower Kingdon in nearby Alverdiscott have been discounted because there is no evidence that either of them was a medieval manor or had any connection with the Priory. Whilst a more recent discovery, [IPM John Wibbury], associates 'the prior of Frithelstock' with land in 'Higher Kyngdon', it remains unclear whether this refers to Higher Kingdon in the parish of Alverdiscott.

hills in the region might have been named Kingdon at one time or another – even though none of them are called that now.[102] Like Kyngdon Manor, they might have been renamed, and their original identities forgotten. Although unlikely, this explanation cannot be discounted, especially given the proximity of Frithelstock to the main population centres of the Kingdon family. *Retain – with reservations.*

So, where was Kingdon? The above survey narrows the choice to two distinct locations:

- The farm now known as Kendon, on the east side of Dartmoor in Devon.
- Somewhere in North Devon, perhaps in the vicinity of Alverdiscott or Frithelstock, but now lost and long forgotten.

In the absence of further evidence, that's as far as this analysis will take us, I suggest.

How did the Kingdons survive and prosper in feudal society?

Consider a society having the following features:

- The social structure is determined by the extended family system.
- The social laws are determined by the extended family system. In particular, there is no legitimacy outside marriage, and there is no marriage outside a narrowly-defined social class.
- All habitation, and most migration, is determined by the extended family system. In particular, when a woman marries she leaves her parental home in order to become another member of her husband's parental home, a phenomenon known as 'patrilocal exogamy'.
- All commerce, and most employment, is determined by the extended family system. In particular, all transactions are subject to negotiation, and the most valuable commodity is influence, that is, 'Who you know'.
- Consequently, over many centuries there is high social stability, low social mixing, and zero social mobility.

Readers will recognise all of these features in the preceding narrative. They are also a fair description of traditional and even contemporary Indian society, as I have often observed during my first-hand experience

102 [Battle of Cynuit] pp.20-21.

of the country that spans more than three decades. As it is said, 'The past is a foreign country: they do things differently there.'[103] This analogy has been a vital guide that has enabled me to understand the medieval feudal system and thereby explain how its citizens – the Kingdons, in particular – survived and prospered. Indeed, the believability of the resulting narrative depends on it.

So, how *did* the Kingdons survive and prosper in feudal society? ASK puts it rather well:

> The Kingdons never pretend to be a noble family. Roger of Quethiock was an extensive landowner, and the John Kyngdon who went to East Leigh, Coldridge, probably on his marriage in 1563, was said to have been given his house by relations in Cornwall, and to have owned most of the village. Between 1329 and 1681 there were Kingdons who were Members of Parliament for constituencies in Cornwall, Devon and elsewhere. They appear in the registers of Oxford and Cambridge Universities and of Lincolns Inn. Several became barristers and one Recorder of Bristol after taking silk. Among the clerics was one bishop; there are Deputy Lieutenants and one or two Privy Councillors.
>
> These however, are the exceptions and are heavily outnumbered by the Kingdons who have served long and faithfully as parish priests, doctors or in some branch of trade and commerce. Some Kingdons have known poverty, or very near it, particularly those from North Devon, but even with these, reading Wills and other records it is impossible not to be struck by a determination on the part of parents to see that their sons 'learned a trade' and did it thoroughly through apprenticeships. This in time brought its own rewards.[104]

In a word, the Kingdons were 'yeomen', and proud of it. Perhaps we still are.[105]

---

103 L P Hartley, *The Go-Between* (1953).

104 [Kingdon Family Second Look] p.4.

105 This might also explain how I came to be born and brought up in Yeovil.

Honed over centuries, has this Kingdon self-image resulted in any distinctive personality traits? Is there a 'typical Kingdon'? Robert Stephen Hawker, the Vicar of Morwenstow, wrote of his brother-in-law that 'he is a Kingdon and I know not a word so expressive of what I call brutishness of mind.'[106] But maybe this says more about Hawker than his subject. And we have to be careful not to confuse what has been passed down in the genes with what has been picked up in the home. After all, with each succeeding generation an ancestor's genes are effectively diluted by another 50%, so that over the c.28 generations between Ælfric of Shapley and Skerraton and me the cumulative dilution has been $1/2^{28}$, or 0.0000004%. That is, Ælfric's contribution to my genotype is negligible, and if we only ever take account of one side of a family then it is clearly nonsense to attribute any particular characteristic to heredity. Cultural traits and attitudes are another matter, of course.

Who held Trehunsey before the Kingdons?

I have noted that, following the breakdown of the feudal system, a person needed access and influence amongst the big beasts in order to acquire his first little freeholding. By 'big beasts' I mean powerful landowners such as the Carminows, wealthy traders such as the Lovecokes, religious houses such as Plympton Priory, and noble families such as the Earls of Devon. Trehunsey would have been acquired by the Kingdons either directly from one of these big beasts, or indirectly from some lesser mortal while under the patronage and protection of one or more of the big beasts. So, if we want to find out who held Trehunsey before the Kingdons, we should start with the lists of landholdings of the big beasts.

Before its tenure by the Kingdons, the only known reference to Trehunsey is the clerical record of William de Trehunsy, who was Rector of Huntsham between 1308 and 1326.[107]

There is no record of Trehunsey amongst the landholdings of the Carminows; they got very close, however. They held the manor of Tregrill in the neighbouring parish of Menheniot, probably acquired together with Boconnoc and other lands when Sir John Carminow married the heiress

106 [Hawker of Morwenstow] p.182; [Kingdon Family Second Look] p.121.

107 [Stapledon Register] p.223; [Grandisson Register I] p.21; [Kingdon Family] p.9; p.10; p.12. Huntsham is a few miles north of Tiverton.

of Glynn.[108] And in 1381 his grandson Sir Ralph Carminow acquired from Thomas Payn and Isabella his wife '15 messuages, 3 mills, 8 acres of land, 35 acres of wood in Treyage, Boterdoun, Westquedyk, & Penacadek & the advowson of the church of Quedyk.'[109] 'Treyage' may be Trago Mills, a few miles west of Liskeard, and a few miles north of Boconnoc. 'Boterdoun' is likely to be Butterdon Mill in Menheniot. This is on the River Tiddy, directly upstream from the site of Trehunsey Mills; which in turn is the obvious candidate for 'Westquedyk' (West Quethiock). Despite strenuous efforts on my part, 'Penacadek' cannot be located.[110] As for the advowson of the church of 'Quedyk' (Quethiock), it appears that this was held already by the Haccombe family.[111] One can only wonder how Sir Ralph Carminow reacted when he discovered that he'd been defrauded by Thomas Payn and Isabella his wife. In any case he didn't have long to worry about it, because in 1386 he met with a fatal hunting accident, being pulled over a cliff by a brace of greyhounds.[112] His little memorial brass, which is probably the oldest in Cornwall, is at the foot of the pulpit in Menheniot church.[113] Subsequently Trehunsey Mills and Penacadek must have been acquired by the Kingdons, because they are both named in the 1557 division of the estate of Thomas Kyngdon of Trehunsey.

As well as the advowson of the church of Quethiock, the Haccombes and their heirs the Archdeknes are known to have held the manor of Penpoll in the parish of Quethiock, plus several estates in the adjacent parish of St Ive.[114] In due course the Archdekne heiress married Sir Hugh Courtenay, a younger brother of the Earl of Devon, who thereby acquired the Haccombe estate. Sir Hugh's son and namesake married one of the

---

108 [Extinct Cornish Families II]. From [Domesday] it appears that Tregrill was first associated with Boconnoc and Glynn in the 1086 holdings of Osfrith of Okehampton. There are no known records of the landholdings of the Glynn family, however.

109 [Cornwall Feet of Fines II] p.10 n.718.

110 These efforts include interpreting 'Penacadek' as 'Cadoc's head' and accordingly searching for it in or near Quethiock. But there is no trace of it, even amongst the names of the fields of the Coryton Estate, see [CY/6705].

111 [Haccombe III] p.324.

112 [Extinct Cornish Families II].

113 [Brasses of Cornwall] p.87.

114 [Cornwall Feet of Fines I] p.423 n.680; pp.441-444 n.693.

Carminow co-heiresses, adding Boconnoc to the collection. But none of them ever held Trehunsey, or married a Kingdon.

In 1431 a consortium headed by the Earl of Warwick acquired over forty parcels of land in Cornwall, including ten in the parish of Menheniot.[115] By this time, of course, Roger Kyngdon was in residence in Trehunsey, and Johanna his wife was producing their legitimate male heir with ten to spare. Nevertheless it is clear that the big beasts continued to prowl all around.

Then there are the religious houses. Recent painstaking research enables us to eliminate the Cornish Priories from our enquiries.[116] Their closest acquisition was Lambest in Menheniot, which was held by St Germans Priory. Further afield, the Bishop of Exeter held lands in Cornwall, but none in Quethiock.[117] Tavistock Abbey, likewise. As for the other religious houses in Devon and beyond, few of them strayed across the Tamar. There is one notable exception, however: Plympton Priory. In the record of the 1291-1292 taxation of Pope Nicholas IV, the following intriguing entry identifies the secular landholding of Plympton Priory in Cornwall:

> Item, in Cornubia, in Decanatu de Estwyvelshire, et Poudre,–
> Aput Tredendale, Cymbe Hendre, Tredenec, et Coleforde
> Trenystone, que taxantur xls. viijd.[118]

My translation:

> In the Cornwall Deaneries of East Wivelshire and Powder,–
> At Tredendale, Cymbe Hendre, Tredenec, and Coleforde
> (and) Trenystone, which are taxed 40s 8d

'Tredendale' is likely to be Tregondale in Menheniot, which is known to have been held by Plympton Priory, and later by the Chivertons.[119] It is close to Trehunsey, on the other side of the River Tiddy. 'Cymbe Hendre' I shall return to. 'Tredenec' and 'Coleforde' are unknown. It is tempting to map them to Tredinnick and Colliford respectively, but these are places in West Wivelshire, not East. 'Trenystone' might be Tresanton in the parish of St Just-in-Roseland of the Deanery of Powder, but I wouldn't bet on it.

115 [Cornwall Feet of Fines II] pp.163-164 n.991.

116 [History of Cornwall II] p.141 (Bodmin); p.185 (St Germans); p.209 (Launceston); p.287 (Tywardreath).

117 [History of Cornwall II] p.23.

118 [Bronescombe Quivil Registers] p.478.

119 [Magna Britannia 3] pp.212-227, Menheniot.

Back to 'Cymbe Hendre'. Is 'Cymbe' an abbreviated reference to the pre-Roman British king variously known as Kynobellinus, Kymbelinus, Cunobelinus, Cunobelin, Cunobeline, Cymbeline, or Cynfelyn?[120] 'Hendre' is easier: it is based on '*Hen* = old and *tre* = steading', which turns out to be 'one of the comparatively few cases where the qualifying adjective precedes the noun in Cornish place-names.'[121] This suggests that, if we were to re-order these word fragments in a proper Cornish fashion, we would get 'Tre-hen-cymbe': which may (or may not) sound like 'Trehunsey' if said with proper Cornish indifference to the usual norms of pronunciation. This might seem far-fetched, but it's not as bad as the suggestion that Trehunsey = Trechunsey = '?Cunsie's dwelling', which puts a *Cornish* prefix on a *Saxon* name (meaning, apparently, 'bold victory').[122] But, again, I wouldn't put any money on either interpretation.

If indeed Trehunsey was held by Plympton Priory then the Kingdons would have lived there as tenants, not owners. But what would have happened after the Dissolution of the Monasteries in 1539? Presumably the Kingdons would have continued as *de facto* owner-occupiers, but feeling rather insecure about it. After all, the Dissolution must have triggered a spectacular feeding-frenzy amongst the big beasts of the day. Maybe the family foresaw the danger and made contingency plans that led ultimately to the acquisition of East Leigh in 1563? This seems plausible enough. There is a fundamental problem with all this speculation, however. Nearly all of the charters and deeds of Plympton Priory were lost in the seventeenth century, as a result of which there is a great dearth of evidence. 'Whereof one cannot speak, thereof one must be silent.'[123]

Choughs or magpies?

This is another of ASK's headings, and it refers to the ongoing debate about the identity of the three birds in the Kingdon coat of arms.[124] The reason this identity matters is because it turns out that the basic design

120 See, for example, [Cunobeline]. The switch from hard-C to soft-C pronunciation happened between the third and sixth centuries, see [Hard and Soft C].

121 [Cornwall Feet of Fines I] p.xx n.8.

122 [Glossary of Cornish Names] p.162; p.155; p.40; [Kingdon Family] p.17.

123 Ludwig Wittgenstein, *Tractatus Logico-Philosophicus* (1922) n.7.

124 [Kingdon Family] pp.130-133; [Kingdon Family Second Look] pp.76-77.

of a chevron with three birds has been used by many families.[125] The following notes summarise my investigations into the heraldic aspects of the Kingdon family history.

- From the outset it must be stated that there is no record that any coat of arms depicting three birds (of whatever species) was ever granted by any serving monarch to any member of the Kingdon family. As a consequence, heraldry is not a reliable guide to the family history, and it must be treated with great caution.
- *If* a coat of arms depicting three birds was ever granted by a serving monarch to a member of the Kingdon family then the most likely recipient would have been Edward Kyngdon, the Yeoman of the Crown. Equally, given Edward's permanent office in the royal court, even if he *hadn't* been granted a coat of arms then he might well have felt the need to create one of his own.
- The c.1471 monumental brass in Quethiock church commemorating Edward's parents is set in a granite slab which also has four small shield-shaped indentations, presumably intended for metal plates depicting coats of arms. These plates have been lost and there is no record of their designs.
- A late fifteenth-century stained glass window in St Kew church depicts a coat of arms with a chevron and three birds, impaled with those of Carminow. The birds have black and white patches, but from their relatively long beaks, long legs, short tails, and webbed feet, it is clear that they are 'seapies' (oystercatchers) rather than magpies.[126] Research by the team that undertook the recent restoration of the window indicates that this coat of arms belongs to the Pentire family rather than the Kingdons.[127] Indeed, it is known that the Pentires lived in that part of North Cornwall at the time, and that one of their number married a Carminow; which on both counts is more than can be said for the Kingdons.

---

125 See, for example, [Devon Armory] pp.46-50; pp.101-103. The chevron with three birds can be found in many places, for example, in two of the quarterings of the Grenville shield illustrated on the frontispiece of [Visitation of Cornwall], where they are attributed to the Tredignie family. The birds in the Tredignie coat of arms are said to be 'Cornish choughs', see [Magna Britannia 3] pp.cxviii-clxxiv, Tredignie.

126 [Kingdon Family Second Look] p.92.

127 [St Kew Window]; [Armory of Western Counties] p.66.

- The earliest reliable record of the Kingdon coat of arms is from notes made by John Hooker, parliamentary representative for Exeter in the sixteenth century. It reads, 'Quetheok. Kingdon: Arg: a cheffron sa: bet: 3 pies proper.'[128] That is, a black chevron and three magpies on a silver background, unambiguously associated with the Kingdons of Quethiock. In the absence of any evidence of a royal grant, this record takes precedence.
- The c.1596 memorial to Robert Trencreeke and Anis his wife in St Erme church depicts the Kingdon coat of arms quartered with those of Vivian. The birds are described as magpies.[129]
- At Kilworthy near Tavistock there are several eighteenth-century wooden panels on which are painted many coats of arms depicting the marital alliances of the Glanville and Manaton families, including one which impales Manaton with Kingdon. This is John Manaton who married Margery, the sister of John Kyngdon of Trehunsey. The birds are described as magpies.[130]
- In the south window of the Exeter church of St Martin's there is a depiction in stained glass of the coats of arms of the Bishop of Exeter, and of the Lacy, Coliford, and Kingdon families. Three of these may be associated with one another, as Edmund Lacy was Bishop of Exeter between 1420 and 1455, while John Colyforde was admitted as chaplain to Exeter St John's Hospital in 1451.[131] The Kingdon coat of arms (with magpies) looks completely out of place, however. ASK expresses a number of misgivings about this window, to which I would add the casual observation that it seems much too well-preserved to be original.[132] Indeed, I am inclined to agree with the view of a local historian who says that 'the window on the south side has the coat of arms of the Kingdon family, probably donated by 'Iron' Sam Kingdon.'[133] That would figure: 'Iron' Sam had a rubbing of the Quethiock brass, and he favoured

128 [Armory of Western Counties] p.86; [Kingdon Family] p.130.

129 [Brasses of Cornwall] pp.57-58; [Kingdon Family Second Look] p.92.

130 [Coat of Arms at Kilworthy] p.319; [Kingdon Family Second Look] p.133.

131 [Lacy Register I] p.361.

132 [Kingdon Family Second Look] pp.123-124; p.132.

133 [St Martins Church].

magpies over choughs, so clearly he was keen on ancestry and heraldry; and his office just happened to be in Cathedral Yard, from where he could observe the ongoing restoration of St Martin's, and be on hand to make a timely and generous contribution.[134] To be clear, in my opinion most or all of the window is a nineteenth-century fake.

- The Exeter Guildhall also has a stained glass window with the Kingdon coat of arms. The window is nineteenth century, so the identity of the birds is irrelevant. (As you might have guessed, they're not magpies.)[135]
- Finally, there's the Kingdon family motto, *Regis donum gratum bonum*. In the preceding narrative I suggested that this might be an appreciative acknowledgement of the relatively easy lives enjoyed by Ælfric and his descendants. But now I'm more inclined to agree with my relative Lorna Kingdon who remarked recently that she never thought it was anything other than wordplay.[136] If so then this would have been perpetrated by the Kingdons of Launcells when they compiled their entry for a genealogical directory.[137] In any case, how could they have known about Ælfric of Shapley and Skerraton?

To answer ASK's dilemma: clearly, the birds are magpies, not choughs; as indeed befits a family that has far more reason to identify with the rural hinterland of Devon than the barren coastline of Cornwall.[138] As for whether heraldry has taught us anything new and useful about the history of the Kingdon family: the answer is no.

---

134 [Kingdon Family Second Look] p.107; p.123.

135 [Kingdon Family Second Look] p.132.

136 Presumably this wordplay would have involved supplementing the translation of *Regis* with the first three letters of *donum*. Lorna's grandfather Frank Hawker Kingdon was the third cousin of my grandfather William Napier Kingdon, which makes us fifth cousins, see [Kingdon Family] p.148 Chart II; p.156 Chart VI.

137 [Kingdon Family] p.131. Launcells is near to Bridgerule.

138 Magpies are a common sight on the fringes of Dartmoor, while choughs are reputed to inhabit Cornish sea-cliffs. That said, less than two miles west-southwest of Kendon there is a narrow ravine, cut by tin miners in ancient times, known as Chough, Chow, or Chaw Gully, 'and so named from the rare Cornish bird associated with the spirit of King Arthur', according to [Crossing's Dartmoor] p.250.

Afterword

I have described the origin of the Kingdons, and explored the principal doubts constraining this story. The main caveat is that the Kingdons of whom I speak are precisely those who can prove their descent from Roger Kyngdon of Trehunsey: and that's a group of people which might not even exist. We might have all emerged from a forgotten mound somewhere in the wilds of North Devon.

There are several weak areas in this narrative which could be addressed by further research. Are the Kingdons under-represented in the court records because their unusual name was systematically altered to something more recognisable? Did the mining industry associated with the stannary towns of Plympton and Liskeard leave any early records? Is there really no trace of who held Trehunsey before the Kingdons? Where is Penacadek, and Cymbe Hendre? How did John Kingdon of Coldridge acquire East Leigh? And what is it about heraldry that leads people to devise their own false trails of imaginary evidence?

'The land of my fathers is dear to me.' Where is this land? For me it was always Bridgerule, the only Devon village to extend west of the Tamar, its church and churchyard overfilled with the memorials of Kingdon ancestors. But I know now that the land of my fathers is much closer to home. That sounds rather twee and sentimental; it also happens to be true. By chance or fate, a few years ago I moved to a cottage on the edge of Dartmoor, just like Kendon, but a dozen miles to the west. Thus it is that my sun now rises over the same bleak moor where the sun of my ancestors once set. Yes: I've come home.

Acknowledgements

My thanks to Kevin Barnes, Angela Bavidge, Robin Boon, Mark Charter, Peter Claughton, Paul Copleston, David Cornforth, Ian Ford, Roshan Forouhi, Tom Greeves, Peter Holden, Arjun Kingdon, Geeta Kingdon, Lorna Kingdon, Robert Kingdon, Janet Lourens, Jo Mattingly, Nicholas Orme, Mark Robinson, Michelle Scott Tucker, Christian Stevens, and Michael Swift, for their comments on an earlier draft of the text.

Abbreviations

ASK	A S Kingdon, author of [Kingdon Family Second Look]
b.	Born (in a given year)
c.	*Circa*, around (a given year)
da.	Daughter
ed(s).	Editor(s)
FBK	F B Kingdon, author of [Kingdon Family]
m.	Married (a named person and/or in a given year)
mem.	Membrane number
n.	Note, section, or edition number
nn.	Note, section, or edition numbers (range)
OE	Old English
p.	Page number
pers. comm.	Personal communication
pp.	Page numbers (range)
Rev	Reverend
s.	Son
TRE	*Tempore Regis Eduardi*, in the time of King Edward
vol.	Volume number

References and resources

[123M/TB60] *All Saints Day 1269 Agreement Between Henry, Abbot of Bukfestr' and convent, and…*, http://discovery.nationalarchives.gov.uk/details/rd/03a9f282-f8f1-472e-a587-60cf7e399f0b.

[Armory of Western Counties] Rev Sabine Baring-Gould and Robert Twigge, *An Armory of the Western Counties* (1898), https://archive.org/details/anarmorywestern00twiggoog.

[Battle of Cynuit] Nick Arnold, *The Site of the Battle of Cynuit 878*, Report and Transactions of the Devonshire Association vol.145 (2013) pp.7-30, [DHC].

[Blanchminster's Charity] Richard William Goulding, *Records of the Charity known as Blanchminster's Charity* (1898), [CRO].

[Brantyngham Register I] Rev Francis Charles Hingeston-Randolph, ed., *The Register of Thomas de Brantyngham, Bishop of Exeter* Part I (1901), https://archive.org/details/registerofthomas01hinguoft.

[Brantyngham Register II] Rev Francis Charles Hingeston-Randolph, ed., *The Register of Thomas de Brantyngham, Bishop of Exeter* Part II (1906), https://archive.org/details/registerofthomas02hing.

[Brasses of Cornwall] Edwin Hadlow Wise Dunkin, *Monumental Brasses of Cornwall* (1882, reprinted 1970), [DHC].

[Bronescombe Quivil Registers] Rev Francis Charles Hingeston-Randolph, ed., *The Registers of Walter Bronscombe and Peter Quivil, Bishops of Exeter* (1889), https://archive.org/details/registerswalter01hinggoog.

[Chittlehampton] Rev J H B Andrews, *Chittlehampton Parish Magazine* (1947-), http://genuki.cs.ncl.ac.uk/DEV/Chittlehampton/HistArticles.html.

[Chiverton Book of Obits V] Peter L Hull, *Thomas Chiverton's Book of Obits* Part V, Devon and Cornwall Notes and Queries vol.33 (1976) pp.277-282 n.141, [DHC].

[Cistercian Houses] Joshua Brooking Rowe, *Contributions to a History of the Cistercian Houses of Devon* (1878), https://archive.org/details/contributionstoh00roweuoft.

[Close Rolls EdII 1318-1323] *Calendar of the Close Rolls, Edward II* 1318-1323 (1895), https://archive.org/details/cu31924091068985.

[Coat of Arms at Kilworthy] John James Alexander, *The Coat of Arms at Kilworthy*, Devon and Cornwall Notes and Queries vol.13 (1924-1925) pp.316-322 n.288, [DHC].

[Copleston] *Copleston Family History*, http://copleston.net/index.htm.

[Cornish Wills] Nicholas Orme, *Cornish Wills 1342-1540*, Devon and Cornwall Record Society New Series vol.50 (2007), [DHC].

[Cornwall Feet of Fines I] Joseph Hambley Rowe, ed., *Cornwall Feet of Fines* vol.I, Devon and Cornwall Record Society Old Series vol.10 (1914), https://archive.org/details/publications81devo.

[Cornwall Feet of Fines II] Joseph Hambley Rowe, ed., *Cornwall Feet of Fines* vol.II, Devon and Cornwall Record Society Old Series vol.11 (1950), [DHC].

[CP 25/1/44/64] *Feet of Fines: CP 25/1/44/64*, www.medievalgenealogy.org.uk/fines/abstracts/CP_25_1_44_64.shtml.

[CRO] Cornwall Record Office, http://www.cornwall.gov.uk/community-and-living/records-archives-and-cornish-studies/.

[Crossing's Dartmoor] William Crossing, *Crossing's Guide to Dartmoor* (1912, David & Charles edition 1965), [DHC].

[Cunobeline] https://en.wikipedia.org/wiki/Cunobeline.

[CY/6705] *Plan of Lands Belonging to John Tillie Coryton in Quethiock* map and tithe database, [CRO].

[Devon Armory] J W Benson, *A Devon Armory* manuscript, [DHC].

[Devon Book of Fees] Rev Oswald Joseph Reichel, *The Earlier Sections of 'Testa Nevil' relating to Devon*, Report and Transactions of the Devonshire Association vol.37 (1905) pp.410-456, https://archive.org/details/reportandtransa20artgoog.

[Devon Eyre 1238] Henry Summerson, ed., *Crown Pleas of the Devon Eyre of 1238*, Devon and Cornwall Record Society New Series vol.28 (1985), [DHC].

[Devon Lay Subsidy 1332] Audrey M Erskine, ed., *The Devon Lay Subsidy of 1332*, Devon and Cornwall Record Society New Series vol.14 (1969), [DHC].

[Devon Surnames] David Postles, *English Surnames Series VI: The Surnames of Devon* (1995), [DHC].

[DHC] Devon Heritage Centre, https://www.swheritage.org.uk/devon-archives.

[Domesday] *Domesday Book* online facility, http://opendomesday.org/.

[Domesday Devon Notes] Caroline and Frank Thorn, eds., *Domesday Book Phillimore Devon Notes* version 1a, https://hydra.hull.ac.uk/resources/hull:535.

[Exeter Accounts] Margery Rowe and John M Draisey, eds., *The Receivers' Accounts of the City of Exeter 1304-1353*, Devon and Cornwall Record Society New Series vol.32 (1989), [DHC].

[Exeter College Register] Rev Charles William Boase, *Register of Exeter College, Oxford* (1894), https://archive.org/details/registrumcollegi00exetrich.

[Extinct Cornish Families II] William Cecil Wade, *Extinct Cornish Families* Part II, Transactions of the Plymouth Institution and Devon and Cornwall Natural History Society (1890-1891), http://patp.us/reading/cornish2.aspx.

[Fine Rolls III] *Calendar of the Fine Rolls, Edward II* vol.III (1912), https://archive.org/details/calendaroffinero03greauoft.

[Fine Rolls VI] *Calendar of the Fine Rolls, Edward III* vol.VI (1921), https://dcms.lds.org/delivery/DeliveryManagerServlet?dps_pid=IE98586.

[Fine Rolls IX] *Calendar of the Fine Rolls, Richard II* vol.IX (1926), https://dcms.lds.org/delivery/DeliveryManagerServlet?dps_pid=IE186266.

[Frithelstock Priory] R Perse Chope, *Frithelstock Priory*, Report and Transactions of the Devonshire Association vol.61 (1929) pp.167-191, [DHC].

[Glossary of Cornish Names] Rev John Bannister, *A Glossary of Cornish Names* (1871), https://archive.org/details/glossaryofcornis00bann.

[Grandisson Register I] Rev Francis Charles Hingeston-Randolph, ed., *The Register of John de Grandisson, Bishop of Exeter* Part I (1894), https://archive.org/details/theregisterofjoh01exetuoft.

[Grandisson Register III] Rev Francis Charles Hingeston-Randolph, ed., *The Register of John de Grandisson, Bishop of Exeter* Part III (1899), https://archive.org/details/registerofjohnde00cath.

[Haccombe III] Albert William Searley, *Haccombe* Part III, Report and Transactions of the Devonshire Association vol.52 (1920) pp.310-326, https://archive.org/details/ReportTransactionsOfTheDevonshireAssociationVol521920.

[Hard and Soft C] https://en.wikipedia.org/wiki/Hard_and_soft_C.

[Hawker of Morwenstow] Piers Brendon, *Hawker of Morwenstow: Portrait of a Victorian Eccentric* (1975), [DHC].

[History of Buckfast Abbey] Dom Adam Hamilton, *History of St Mary's Abbey of Buckfast* (1906), https://archive.org/details/historyofstmarys00hami.

[History of Cornwall II] Nicholas Orme, *A History of the County of Cornwall* vol.II (2010), http://www.biodiversitylibrary.org/item/122349#page/11/mode/1up.

[History of Liskeard] John Allen, *History of the Borough of Liskeard and its Vicinity* (1856), https://books.google.co.uk/books?id=YuUGAAAAQAAJ.

[History of Plympton] Joshua Brooking Rowe, *A History of the Borough of Plympton Erle* (1906), https://archive.org/details/ahistoryborough00rowegoog.

[History of Totnes 1] Hugh Robert Watkin, *The History of Totnes Priory & Medieval Town* vol.1 (1914), https://archive.org/details/cu31924091781322.

[History of Totnes 2] Hugh Robert Watkin, *The History of Totnes Priory & Medieval Town* vol.2 (1914), [DHC].

[IPM John Wibbury] King's College London, *Mapping the Medieval Countryside* (2014), http://www.inquisitionspostmortem.ac.uk/view/inquisition/22-137.

[IPM Margaret de Courtenay] M C B Dawes, H C Johnson, M M Condon, C A Cook and H E Jones, *Inquisitions Post Mortem, Richard II, File 70*, Calendar of Inquisitions Post Mortem vol.17 Richard II (1988) pp.1-12, http://www.british-history.ac.uk/inquis-post-mortem/vol17/pp1-12.

[JUST 1/175] *Devon eyre of 1244, roll of civil and crown pleas, jury calendar and essoins*, http://discovery.nationalarchives.gov.uk/details/r/C4292884.

[Keynedon Barton] Robert E Waterhouse, *Keynedon Barton, Sherford, Kingsbridge*, Proceedings of the Devon Archaeological Society vol.58 (2000) pp.127-200, [DHC].

[Kingdon Family] Frederick Buckingham Kingdon, *The Kingdon Family* (1932), http://www.idealectic.com/idealectic/Genealogy.htm.

[Kingdon Family Second Look] Albert Sidney Kingdon, *The Kingdon Family – A Second Look* (1974-1977), [DHC].

[King's Serjeants] John Horace Round, *The King's Serjeants and Officers of State* (1911), https://archive.org/details/kingsserjeantsof00rounuoft.

[Lacy Register I] Rev Francis Charles Hingeston-Randolph, ed., *The Register of Edmund Lacy, Bishop of Exeter* Part I (1909), https://archive.org/details/09934315.1323.emory.edu.

[Launceston Cartulary] Peter L Hull, ed., *The Cartulary of Launceston Priory*, Devon and Cornwall Record Society New Series vol.30 (1987), [DHC].

[Magna Britannia 3] Daniel Lysons and Samuel Lysons, *Magna Britannia* vol.3 (1814), http://www.british-history.ac.uk/magna-britannia/vol3.

[Magna Carta] *Magna Carta* 1225 revision, http://www.intriguing-history.com/magna-carta-translation-1225/.

[Medieval Schools] Nicholas Orme, *Medieval Schools: From Roman Britain to Renaissance England* (2006), https://books.google.co.uk/books?id=5mzTVODUjB0C.

[New History of Buckfast Abbey] Dom John Stephan, *Buckfast Abbey: A New History from 1018-1968* (1970), [DHC].

[Patent Rolls EdI 1272-1281] *Calendar of the Patent Rolls, Edward I* 1272-1281 (1901), https://archive.org/details/calendarofpatent01grea.

[Patent Rolls Search] *Calendar of the Patent Rolls (1216-1452)* online search facility, http://sdrc.lib.uiowa.edu/patentrolls/search.html.

[Silver Mines] Stephen Rippon, Peter Claughton and Chris Smart, *Mining in a Medieval Landscape: The Royal Silver Mines of the Tamar Valley* (2009), [DHC].

[Stafford Register Index] Rev Francis Charles Hingeston-Randolph, ed., *The Register of Edmund Stafford, Bishop of Exeter* Index and Abstract (1886), https://archive.org/details/registerofedmund00cathuoft.

[Stanborough 100 TN] Rev Oswald Joseph Reichel, *The Hundred of Stanborough or Dippeforda, A Supplement to Testa de Nevil*, Report and Transactions of the Devonshire Association vol.45 (1913) pp.198-207, https://archive.org/details/ReportTransactionsOfTheDevonshireAssociationVol451913.

[Stannaries] George Randall Lewis, *The Stannaries: A Study of the Medieval Tin Miners of Cornwall and Devon* (1908), http://socserv2.socsci.mcmaster.ca/econ/ugcm/3ll3/lewis/index.html.

[Stannary of Tavistock] Herbert Patrick Reginald Finberg, *The Stannary of Tavistock*, Report and Transactions of the Devonshire Association vol.81 (1949) pp.155-184, [DHC].

[Stapledon Register] Rev Francis Charles Hingeston-Randolph, ed., *The Register of Walter de Stapledon, Bishop of Exeter* (1892), https://archive.org/details/registerofwalter00hing.

[St Kew Window] Joanna Mattingly and Michael Swift, *The Restoration of the Medieval St Kew Window* (2006), https://www.cornishstainedglass.org.uk/mgskew/.

[St Martins Church] David Cornforth, *St Martins Church – Cathedral Close* (2012), http://www.exetermemories.co.uk/em/_churches/stmartins.php.

[Survey of Cornwall] Richard Carew, *The Survey of Cornwall* (1769), https://archive.org/details/surveycornwalla00caregoog.

[Visitation of Cornwall] John Lambrick Vivian, *The Visitation of the County of Cornwall in the Year 1620* (1874), https://archive.org/details/visitationofcoun00sain.